HEMET PUBLIC LIBRARY
510 E. FLORIDA AVE.
HEMET, CA   92543

THE NERVOUS SYSTEM

HEMET PUBLIC LIBRARY
510 E. FLORIDA AVE.
HEMET, CA 92543

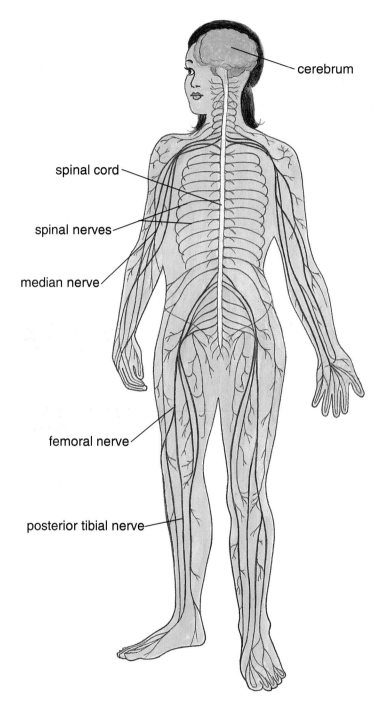

cerebrum

spinal cord

spinal nerves

median nerve

femoral nerve

posterior tibial nerve

The Nervous System

xR 612 S
SILVERSTEIN, ALVIN
   THE NERVOUS SYSTEM

HUMAN BODY SYSTEMS

THE NERVOUS SYSTEM

DR. ALVIN, VIRGINIA, AND ROBERT SILVERSTEIN

TWENTY-FIRST CENTURY BOOKS
A Division of Henry Holt and Company
New York

OCT 0 1 1997
HEMET PUBLIC LIBRARY
510 E. FLORIDA AVE.
HEMET, CA 92543

Twenty-First Century Books
A Division of Henry Holt and Company, Inc.
115 West 18th Street
New York, NY 10011

Henry Holt ® and colophon are trademarks of
Henry Holt and Company, Inc.
Publishers since 1866

Text Copyright © 1994 Dr. Alvin Silverstein, Virginia Silverstein, and Robert Silverstein
Endpaper illustrations Copyright © 1994 Greg Harris
Illustrations Copyright © 1994 Lloyd Birmingham
All rights reserved.
Published in Canada by Fitzhenry & Whiteside Ltd.
195 Allstate Parkway, Markham, Ontario L3R 4T8

Library of Congress Cataloging-in-Publication Data
Silverstein, Alvin.
Nervous system / Alvin, Virginia, and Robert Silverstein.—1st ed.
p. cm. — (Human body systems)
Includes index.
1. Neurophysiology—Juvenile literature. 2. Nervous system—Juvenile literature. [1.Nervous
system.] I. Silverstein, Virginia B. II. Silverstein, Robert A. III. Title. IV. Series.
QP361.5.S538 1994
612.8—dc20 94-25917
CIP
AC

ISBN 0-8050-2835-8
First Edition 1994

Printed in Mexico
All first editions are printed on acid-free paper ∞.
10 9 8 7 6 5 4 3 2

Drawings by Lloyd Birmingham

Photo Credits

Cover: Howard Sochurek/The Stock Market

p. 9: Richard Hutchings/Photo Researchers, Inc.; p. 11: E. R. Degginger/Photo Researchers, Inc.; p. 14: National Library of Medicine/Science Photo Library/Photo Researchers, Inc.; p. 15: Science Photo Library/Photo Researchers, Inc.; p. 25: Jean-Marc Loubat/Agence Vandystadt/Photo Researchers, Inc.; p. 27: Biophoto Associates/Science Source/Photo Researchers, Inc.; p. 30: Alfred Pasieka/Science Photo Library/Photo Researchers, Inc.; p. 33: Edward Drews/Photo Researchers, Inc.; p. 34: SIU/Custom Medical Stock Photo; p. 42: Srulik Haramaty/Phototake NYC; p. 50: Will and Deni McIntyre/Photo Researchers, Inc.; p. 62: Erika Stone/Photo Researchers, Inc.; p. 71: Hank Morgan/Science Source/Photo Researchers, Inc.; p. 74: Jeffery Titcomb/Liaison International; p. 80: Larry Mulvehill/Photo Researchers, Inc.; p. 84: Joseph Nettis/Photo Researchers, Inc.; p. 88: Gregory Ochocki/Photo Researchers, Inc.

CONTENTS

SECTION 1

MESSAGES FOR LIFE

Your body is like a large city. Each of its trillions of cells is a specialist. Each cell works with other cells that specialize in the same job that it does. Together these specialists make up a body system. The many body systems all work together to keep you alive and help you to interact with the world around you.

The people in a city also offer their individual talents to help keep the city functioning. The government of a city tries to coordinate activities and services to keep things going smoothly. In your body, the nervous system coordinates and directs the activities of all the other body systems to keep you healthy.

Like a city, the body has "roads" for transporting materials—the bloodstream and digestive system, for example. It also has communication systems to help coordinate the activities of all the body systems.

The endocrine system is like the postal system of a large city. Glands secrete chemicals called hormones into the blood, and they travel to the parts of the body much as a mail truck carries letters through the streets of the city. But mail service is a rather slow way of sending messages, and so is the endocrine system. A much quicker way to deliver messages in the body is through the nervous system. In a city you can call people on the telephone or fax them messages to give them the latest news or ask them to do something. The information is carried over wires from one part of the city to another.

The "wires" of the nervous system are made up of nerve cells, called **neurons**. Nearly all animals, except the simplest ones, have a nervous system made up of nerve cells. Among the higher animals, vast numbers of nerve cells are grouped together to form a **brain**. The brain is in charge of the nervous system. Other nerve cells are grouped together to form a long cord, known as a **spinal cord**, that runs through the backbone. The spinal cord carries messages back and forth between the body and the brain. It also controls some activities in the body without the brain's input.

The brain and spinal cord act as a sort of "central office." They are called the **central nervous system**. Incoming messages from the sense organs (the eyes, ears, nose, tongue, and skin) are analyzed in your central nervous system to let you know what is going on around you. Then the brain and spinal cord send messages along the nerves to the muscles and other parts of the body, telling them what to do. Nerves also link the brain to most internal organs, so that your central office knows what is going on inside you, too.

Many of the activities of the nervous system involve conscious decisions made in the brain—such as your turning the pages of this book. But many other activities are carried out entirely without awareness or conscious control. Without your nervous system, you would be unable to think or use any of your muscles. You could not move your hands, blink your eyes, sit or stand, swallow, or even breathe.

Your central nervous system interprets what your eyes see when you read and how the pages feel when you turn them.

NERVOUS SYSTEMS IN LOWER ANIMALS

Simple one-celled creatures do not have nervous systems, but they can still respond to the world around them, to a limited degree. The simplest many-celled creatures, the sponges, do not have any specialized nervous system either, and as you might expect, their responses to their environment are very slow and simple.

The first nerve cells are found in the group of coelenterates, which includes the jellyfish and the tentacled hydra, a microscopic animal that lives in ponds. The nerve cells of coelenterates are arranged in a **nerve net**, which is spread through the body of the animal like a fish net. Messages can travel along the nerves in either direction. A single **impulse**, or message, rapidly spreads along the many branches of the net through the entire body. If you touched the tip of one tentacle of a hydra, its whole body might contract (get shorter) in response. This is not a very efficient coordinating system, but it is good enough for these animals to catch their food and respond to many changes in the world about them.

A flatworm is a more highly developed animal than a coelenterate in many ways, and it has a much more efficient nervous system. Not only does it have specialized nerve cells, but it has a central nervous system: a brain and two nerve cords running along the length of its body. These nerve

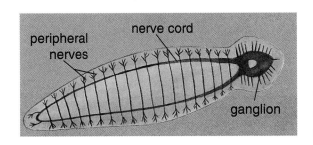

Most flatworms are less than 1 inch (2.5 centimeters) long. Flatworms have a simple but efficient nervous system.

cords are connected by thin nerves so that they look like a ladder. Other nerves branch off from the cords and carry messages to or from various parts of the body. The flatworm's brain relays messages from the worm's two small eyes and other sense cells, and sends them along the "main highways" of the nerve cords to various parts of the body. But in this primitive animal the brain is not really very important in coordinating movements; if a flatworm's head is cut off, it can still move about quite normally. And eventually it grows a new head!

In some of the higher invertebrates (animals without a **backbone**) the central nervous system is quite well developed. The octopus, for example, has a rather large "brain" and is capable of finely controlled movements and complicated behavior. Scientists have taught octopuses to solve simple problems and even to tell the difference between a circle and a square or a small circle and a large one.

An octopus has the most highly developed brain among the invertebrates.

Many insects, too, have both a highly developed central nervous system and very efficient sense organs. Insects' nerve cells lie side-by-side. In some areas the cells are bunched together into masses called **ganglia**, which are almost like brains but much simpler. An insect's brain receives information from the sense organs of the insect's head and directs the body movements, but the brain does not coordinate the actions of the body muscles. If a grasshopper's brain is removed, for example, it can still walk, jump, and even fly. In fact it will jump or fly at the slightest touch or other stimulation. It seems, rather, that the insect's brain works to stop or inhibit any unnecessary movement.

Insects can learn and remember; some, such as bees and ants, can even cooperate with one another to build great "cities" and work together to accomplish tasks that a single insect could not do alone. A bee can do all this with only about 7,000 neurons in its brain; humans have as many as 100 billion neurons!

THE VERTEBRATE NERVOUS SYSTEM

Only vertebrates (animals with a backbone) have real brains and spinal cords. Among the backboned animals, fish have the simplest brains. A fish's brain is only a little bigger than a fish's eye. Larger animals, such as elephants and whales, need larger brains. A whale's brain is much bigger than a human's—a sperm whale's brain, for example, weighs six times as much as an adult human brain. But compared to the size of our bodies, a human's brain is proportionately much bigger. It isn't just the size of the brain that is important. The size and importance of the different parts of the brain help to determine an animal's intelligence.

All vertebrate brains have some similarities. Scientists believe that fish were the ancestors of amphibians and reptiles, and birds and mammals

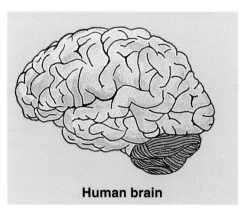 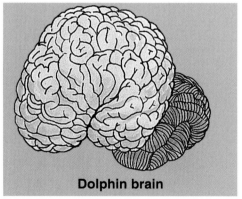

Human brain   **Dolphin brain**

A dolphin brain (right) has numerous folds, similar to a human brain (left). The area controlling a dolphin's hearing is better developed than in a human brain, but the human brain has a larger cerebrum—the center for thought, memory, and personality.

evolved from reptiles; the structures of their brains support this idea. There are three main parts to a vertebrate brain: the **hindbrain**, the **midbrain**, and the **forebrain**.

The hindbrain, which forms a swelling at the head end of the spinal cord, consists of the **pons**, **medulla oblongata**, and the **cerebellum** and has the same basic structure and function in all vertebrates. The pons forms a bridge between the midbrain and the medulla. The medulla controls some automatic functions such as breathing, swallowing, and vomiting. The cerebellum, which helps to control balance and coordinate movements, is larger and more complex in higher animals such as mammals.

The midbrain is the most highly developed part of the brain in primitive vertebrates, such as fish and amphibians. In addition to relaying information up from the lower brain and spinal cord, it contains centers for crude forms of seeing and hearing.

The forebrain makes up only a small part of the brain in these animals. In fact, the forebrain of a fish is largely devoted to processing information from the chemical senses, taste and smell. As animals evolved, the midbrain became less important, and the forebrain, especially the portion called the **cerebrum**, became larger and more important.

Calling someone a "birdbrain" is considered an insult. Actually, though, the bird's brain is the most developed among all the vertebrates except for the mammals. A bird must depend on its keen eyesight to spot food and a safe landing place, and its brain structure reflects those needs. The optic lobes of the midbrain are quite well developed, and a large part of the bulging cerebrum is involved in receiving and processing information from the bird's eyes. Some birds, such as parrots, are quite good at learning tricks and working out various problems.

The cerebrum is what distinguishes mammals from other animals. This "higher brain" receives and processes information both from the sense organs and from the more primitive parts of the brain. It controls and coordinates activities and is the conscious part of the brain, the part involved in thought, reasoning, and decision making.

LEARNING ABOUT THE NERVOUS SYSTEM

Early people did not know anything about the brain, but they did know that the head was important. They knew that someone who was hit in the head could be seriously hurt or even die. In some places, such as in Africa, warriors believed that they would have special powers if they kept the heads of the people that they had killed in battle.

For many years people thought that evil spirits caused illnesses. The spirits got inside a person's head, and the only way to get them out was to cut a hole in the victim's head. A healer's power was believed to be found in the head, too.

Hippocrates

More than 2,000 years ago, Hippocrates and other ancient Greek doctors believed that the brain had the power of thought and understanding. Hippocrates also said that the brain was involved in hearing, smelling, tasting, and the other senses.

But the Greeks did not totally understand the brain. Galen, a famous Greek doctor from the second century A.D., showed that the brain sent messages to the body through the spinal cord and even linked **paralysis** in various parts of the body to damage in specific parts of the central nervous system. But Galen thought that movement was produced when special "animal spirits" filled the muscles of our arms or legs. He also believed that the heart was the body's real control center.

In the mid-1500s, the Belgian anatomist Andreas Vesalius suggested that thoughts and feelings came from the brain, not the heart. A seventeenth-century English doctor, William Harvey, proved that the heart was just a pump for sending blood around the body. People still continued to believe that animals spirits filled muscles to cause movement, though.

A seventeenth-century Dutch scientist named Jan Swammerdam showed that muscles cause movement not by expanding but by contracting. Then, in the 1770s, Luigi Galvani, an Italian scientist, showed that electricity causes muscles to contract. Later other scientists discovered that electricity flows through the nerves.

Luigi Galvani

A German doctor named Franz Gall studied the brain and the skull about 200 years ago. He believed that different parts of the body were controlled by different parts of the brain. Other doctors mapped out many of the centers in the brain that control the activities of the body.

In 1873 an Italian physician, Camillo Golgi, was the first to observe nerve cells after he developed a special stain that darkened the neurons so they could be seen better under a microscope. With an improved version of Golgi's stain, a Spanish scientist named Santiago Ramón y Cajal proved that the whole nervous system was made up of nerve cells.

In the late nineteenth century a German scientist, Walther Hermann Nernst, suggested that messages were carried along nerves by electrochemical reactions. And then in the early 1950s, British scientists Alan Lloyd Hodgkin and Andrew Fielding Huxley were able to describe step-by-step how nerve messages are transmitted.

DID YOU KNOW . . .

One type of fortune-telling called phrenology involves feeling the bumps on a person's head. People used to believe that the shape of different parts of the head can tell a lot about someone's personality.

OUR NERVOUS SYSTEM

The brain and the spinal cord are the central controllers of the nervous system. Together they make up the central nervous system. They are linked to the sense organs, muscles, and other parts of the body by an intricate network of nerves that stretches all through the body. Each of these nerves is a bundle of many tiny, threadlike nerve cells, bound together within a sheath of tissue that is like the insulation around a telephone wire.

The nerves that connect the brain and spinal cord to the parts of the body make up the **peripheral nervous system**. There are two main types of peripheral nerve cells: those that carry messages from the sense organs to the spinal cord and the brain (**sensory nerves**), and those that carry messages from the brain and spinal cord to other parts of the body (**motor nerves**).

Messages travel in only one direction along our nerves, and the same nerve cell does not carry messages both ways at once. Sensory nerves let the central nervous system know what is going on inside and outside the body. Motor nerves tell the muscles to move and the glands to secrete chemicals. They keep the heart beating, the lungs breathing, and the stomach churning.

Some of the messages that the brain sends out to the various parts of the body are things that we consciously think about. Lift your right hand and wave it from side to side. Wiggle your thumb and then stretch your fingers out as far as they will go. You knew exactly what was going on all the time. You could control how far you moved your hand and how fast. You could move one finger at a time or all of them together. Scientists would say that all these actions were under conscious control.

But if we had to think about everything we do before we did it, we would not survive very long. What if you had to think about blinking your eyes or ducking your head if you suddenly spotted a rock flying toward you? What if you had to think about pulling your hand away if you touched a very hot pot? In cases like these the body acts automatically, so fast you really don't have time to think about it until afterward. These automatic actions are coordinated by either the spinal cord or certain parts of the brain. They are called **reflex actions**.

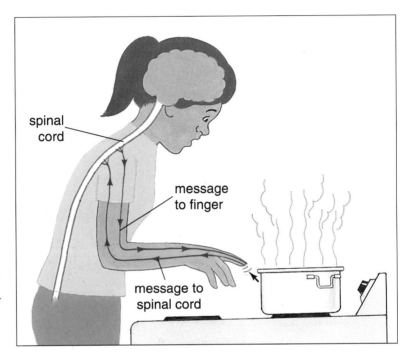

You don't have to make a decision to pull your hand away from a hot pot—the body acts automatically with a reflex action.

Things are constantly happening in the world around us and within our bodies. We never really know about most of the activities that go on inside us. Our stomach and intestines are constantly moving as they digest our food, even when we have not eaten for a long time. The spleen and gallbladder often squeeze in and out, and the blood vessels are widened or narrowed to meet the changing needs of the body. The brain and spinal cord have control over this inner world, too. They coordinate the activities of the heart, the lungs, the stomach and intestines, and the various other organs within our bodies through special sets of motor nerves that together make up the independent, or **autonomic nervous system**.

NERVE CELLS

The brain, spinal cord, and nerves are made up of nerve cells called **neurons**. You can make a rough model of a neuron out of a piece of kite string about a foot (30 centimeters) long. Tie a knot a few inches (8 centimeters) from one end. Unravel both ends of the string so that many loose threads dangle out in all directions.

The knot in your cord represents the **cell body** of the neuron. It has a nucleus and various other structures that are found in typical body cells. The cell body of a neuron is ball shaped, about 0.001 inch (0.025 millimeter) wide. It supplies the rest of the neuron with food materials for energy.

The dangling hairlike threads at the end near the knot in the cord are like the **dendrites** of a neuron. They are branches that carry messages toward the cell body. (*Dendrite* comes from a Greek word meaning "tree.")

The long piece of string extending out from the knot like a tail corresponds to a part of the neuron called the **axon**. There is usually only a single axon in a neuron, and it leads to a cluster of branches called fibrils, or terminal branches, because they are at the end of the axon. Both the axons and dendrites of nerve cells are called **nerve fibers**.

The axon and dendrites of a nerve cell are wrapped in a protective covering. Many nerve fibers, in fact, have two protective sheaths, one inside the other. The inner sheath is called the **myelin sheath**. It is made of a fatty substance and has a shiny white appearance. The outer sheath is made up of living cells and is called the **neurilemma**.

Scientists believe that the fatty myelin sheath may act like the insulation of an electric wire, keeping the nerve messages from interfering with one another. And the neurilemma seems to help a cut nerve fiber grow back together, replacing the parts that have been damaged. Only nerve cells that have a neurilemma can do this.

The neurons in the brain and spinal cord do not have a neurilemma. Indeed, some of them do not have a myelin sheath, either. They are just bare nerve cells. The outer part of the brain is a grayish color because it is mostly bare nerve cells without the white myelin sheath covering. This kind of tissue in the brain and spinal cord is called **gray matter**. **White matter** lies beneath the gray matter in the brain. It is composed of neurons whose nerve fibers are covered by a myelin sheath. In the spinal cord, white matter is on the outside and gray matter is inside.

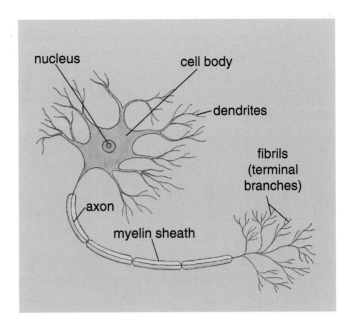

The basic structure of a nerve cell

Some kinds of cells in our bodies grow and multiply. Skin cells are constantly being replaced, as the outer layers die and are rubbed off. Bone cells and blood cells, too, can reproduce themselves. But nerve cells cannot. Through all our lives we have the same nerve cells we had when we were babies. They can grow, but our bodies cannot make any more of them. If a nerve cell dies, it cannot be replaced. Indeed, this is happening all the time, and by the time a person is very old, as many as a quarter of his or her neurons may have died. That is one of the reasons that the brain of an old person may not work as quickly and well as it used to.

Our brains contain between 10 billion and 100 billion neurons. But there are ten times this number of another kind of cell. These are the neuroglia, or **glial cells**. *Glial* comes from a Greek word for "glue." Glial cells help to hold nerve tissue together. They also provide support and protection for nerve cells, help supply the neurons with nutrients, and get rid of neurons that have died.

THE SPINAL CORD

The spinal cord is like a long, thick white rope running down from the bottom of the brain. In the average adult, this cylinder of nerve cells is about 1.5 feet (45 centimeters) long and 1 inch (2.5 centimeters) wide, and it weighs just over 1 ounce (28 grams).

From the outside, the spinal cord looks white. This thick layer of white matter contains nerve fibers that deliver signals to and from the brain. The gray matter of the cord is concentrated inside. It contains the cell bodies of motor neurons that carry signals to the muscles.

Running along the surface of the spinal cord are spinal arteries that provide the cord with its own blood supply. The spine is nestled in a long channel called the vertebral column or backbone, which is made up of individual bones called **vertebrae**.

A few nerves in the head lead straight to the brain, but all of the rest of the nerves in the body lead to the spinal cord first. The spinal cord extends about two-thirds of the way down inside the vertebral column. At regular intervals, large nerves branch out between the vertebrae and go to all parts of the

Individual bones called vertebrae surround the long spinal cord.

body. There are 31 pairs of these **spinal nerves**. Each one contains thousands of both sensory and motor neurons. It is through these nerves that messages travel to and from the spinal cord.

Spinal nerves in the neck area bring messages to and from the head, neck, and hands. Spinal nerves in the chest take care of the chest muscles, skin, and internal organs such as the heart and lungs. Spinal nerves that branch from the lower end of the spinal cord serve the lower part of the body—the stomach area, as well as the legs and feet.

If any of these nerves were injured, a person might become paralyzed; messages could no longer be delivered from the brain and spinal cord to tell the muscles to move the body part serviced by those nerves. If the spinal cord itself were severed or severely damaged, none of the spinal nerves below the point of injury would be able to transmit messages.

The spinal cord is far less complex than the brain, and so its functions are less complicated, too. But they are very important. The spinal cord serves mainly as a relay station. It relays messages to the brain from the sensory nerves, and delivers messages from the brain to the appropriate parts of the body. But the spine also deals with many activities without involving the brain. These are reflexive actions that occur automatically without conscious thought whenever specific messages are sent by the sense organs.

THE BRAIN

Close your eyes and try to "see" something inside your mind—the faces of some people you know or a scene in the country. Try to "hear" some sound you heard sometime before. The scene or sound in your mind almost seems real. These memories are locked up in your brain. The brain is a grayish, jellylike organ about the size of two clenched fists held together, or a little larger than a large grapefruit. It looks like a huge walnut, covered with grooves and folds. The brain is divided into the forebrain, the midbrain, and the hindbrain.

The cerebrum makes up most of the forebrain and, in fact, between 85 and 90 percent of the whole human brain. Most of the brain's work is done here. The centers for sight, sound, taste, smell, and touch, as well as thinking and memory, decision making, and controls for moving various body muscles, are all found in the outermost layer, the **cerebral cortex**.

Nestled between the two halves of the cerebrum are some other important parts of the forebrain. The **thalamus** is the brain's main relay station, sending information on to the cerebral cortex and other parts of the brain. The **hypothalamus** contains many control centers for body functions and also centers for emotions such as anger, fear, and pleasure.

The midbrain and part of the hindbrain make up the **brain stem**. Four tiny **colliculi** in the midbrain correspond to the sight- and sound-analyzing systems in the brains of lower vertebrates. In humans, these midbrain structures help to control the eye muscles and size of the pupils, and to adjust the ears to the amount of sound coming in. It is the colliculi that make you flinch at a loud noise or blink when an insect flies toward you.

The hindbrain is divided into three parts: the pons, medulla oblongata, and cerebellum. The pons is a bridge of nerve fibers in the brain stem, between the midbrain and the medulla. It serves as a relay station linking the medulla with the higher cortical centers.

The medulla oblongata blends into the spinal cord. This inch-long part of the brain is responsible for controlling many of the involuntary actions of the body, such as heartbeat, breathing, and digestion.

The cerebellum is tucked under the cerebrum in the back of the brain. It looks like a smaller version of the cerebrum. It is responsible for coordinating movements in the body and for balance.

The cerebrum might be thought of as the higher brain, because it is best developed only in humans and in the most intelligent animals. The rest of the brain is sometimes called the primitive brain, for it contains the parts that developed first in the history of the animal world.

The average adult brain weighs close to 3 pounds (about 1.3 kilograms). A man's brain is usually somewhat larger than a woman's, but this difference in size has nothing to do with intelligence. In fact, the proportion of brain to body weight is slightly higher in females than in males. Human brains have been getting larger. The average brain today is one-half pound (0.23 kilogram) heavier than the average brain only a century ago.

The brain is so active metabolically that it receives about 17 percent of the blood pumped by the heart and uses about 20 percent of the oxygen consumed, even though it is only 2 percent of the body's weight.

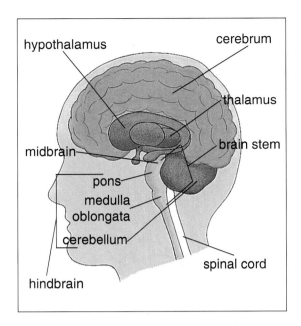

Location of the main parts of the human brain.

ARE BOYS SMARTER THAN GIRLS?

Scientists say that the two sexes are about equal in overall intelligence, but that men may be stronger in some kinds of intelligence and women in other kinds. Even before birth, girls have a larger corpus callosum, the link between the two cerebral hemispheres. In boys the right brain, which is concerned with spatial and mathematical abilities, develops earlier. In girls the left hemisphere develops earlier, and girls tend to be more fluent verbally and develop better fine muscle control. But researchers point out that these differences are only averages.

PROTECTION

The brain and the spinal cord are the most important and carefully protected structures in the whole body. The brain is encased in the skull, or **cranium**, a rigid helmet formed by the cranial bones. Although the skull is solid, it is actually formed from 29 bones, tightly fused together.

The spinal cord is enclosed in a flexible column of bones called vertebrae. There are 33 vertebrae, which are rings of bone that fit snugly into each other. You can feel them if you run your hand down your back. Even though the individual bones, or vertebrae, fit together to provide protection for the spinal cord, you can still bend and turn. And the spinal cord itself is suspended loosely in the vertebral canal so that it is not damaged when the spinal column bends and twists.

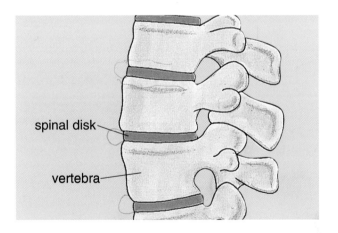

The top 24 vertebrae have soft, rubbery cushions between them. These cushions are called spinal disks, and they are made of a spongy material called cartilage. Spinal disks help reduce the shock your spine has to put up with as you jump and run. The disks also allow a little movement between the vertebrae so that the spine can bend. In addition to protecting the spinal cord, the spine also serves to support the whole skeleton.

The spinal column is flexible, allowing us to bend.

Inside their bony protections, both the brain and the spinal cord are wrapped in a set of three membranes, one inside the other, called the **meninges**. The outermost membrane, the **dura mater**, is a tough, protective casing that lines the inside of the cranium and spinal column. (*Dura* means "hard.") The middle membrane, the **arachnoid membrane**, is thin and delicate like a spiderweb. (*Arachnoid* comes from a Greek word meaning "cobweb.") The innermost membrane, the **pia mater**, forms a soft and delicate covering for the brain and spinal cord. (*Pia* means "tender.") Blood vessels that bring blood to and from the brain and spinal cord pass through this membrane.

There are hollow cavities called ventricles inside the cerebrum. They are connected to a single central ventricle, and this is connected through another ventricle to the hollow center of the spinal cord. **Cerebrospinal fluid**, a clear liquid produced by the brain, is found in the ventricles and the channel inside the spinal cord. It also bathes the space between the inner and middle meninges. Cerebrospinal fluid acts as a cushiony shock absorber and also circulates nutrients that have been filtered out of the blood.

The skin of the scalp that covers the cranium also provides some protection, as does the hair on top of the head.

PERIPHERAL NERVES

The axons and dendrites that branch out from the central nervous system and spread through the body are grouped together into bundles called nerves. Each nerve bundle may contain as many as a million or more individual nerve fibers. Most of the axons in the central nervous system are less than 0.04 inch (1 millimeter) long. In the peripheral nervous system, though, some axons are much longer. Those that extend from the spinal cord to the muscles in the feet, for example, may be 30 to 40 inches (76 to 101 centimeters) long.

Each nerve fiber in a nerve has its own insulating sheath. The bundle of nerve fibers that makes up a nerve is enclosed in another protective sheath. These bundles are in turn grouped into a larger bundle, which is wrapped in still another protective covering. This bundle of bundles is also laced with blood vessels and often contains fat cells. Less than a quarter of the material in a nerve actually consists of nerve cells. More than half is connective tissue and blood vessels, and a quarter is myelin!

Each nerve fiber runs the full length of the nerve. It keeps its own distinct identity, although it may branch and rebranch many times. A nerve is like a large telephone cable, containing many thin insulated wires. Each wire can carry its own independent message, without any interference from the other wires in the cable, and so can each individual nerve fiber in a nerve. The combined action of all the individual messages in a nerve can cause a muscle to move, prompt a gland to secrete its particular chemicals, or bring messages from the senses.

Without its links to the outside world, your brain would be useless—unable to receive information or translate its own messages into actions. The links are provided by the peripheral nerves. These nerves branch out from the brain and spinal cord and run as slender threads through the head, trunk, arms, and legs.

Peripheral nerves are often classified as **cranial nerves** and spinal nerves, depending on whether they emerge from the brain or spinal cord. There are 12 pairs of cranial nerves and 31 pairs of spinal nerves. Some of the cranial nerves bring messages from the eyes, ears, and other sense organs. Others control the action of muscles and glands. The two **olfactory nerves**, which carry smell messages from the nose, emerge directly from the underside of the cerebrum. The **optic nerves**, from the eyes, are connected to the hypothalamus. The rest of the cranial nerves branch off from the brain stem.

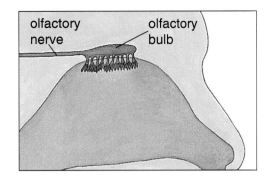

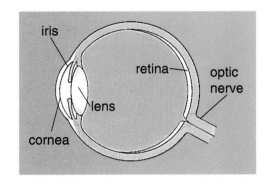

Spinal nerves emerge on both sides of the spinal cord through gaps between two vertebrae. Once outside the cord, the spinal nerves branch into two bundles. One is a motor nerve that contains only motor nerve fibers, transmitting messages from the central nervous system to the outer parts of the body. The other is a sensory nerve that contains only sensory nerve fibers, transmitting messages from the body's senses to the central nervous system. Most of the nerves in the body are **mixed nerves**, containing both motor and sensory fibers.

Scattered through the peripheral nervous system are numerous ganglia, knot-like masses consisting of groups of nerve cell bodies. Most nerve cell bodies that are not in the central nervous system are found in these ganglia. The ganglia allow for some intercommunication among the nerve fibers. In some regions, fibers of peripheral nerves intermix, forming an intricate network called a plexus.

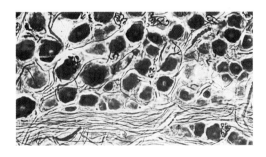

The dark, circular areas in this photo are ganglia.

HOW NERVE MESSAGES TRAVEL

Neurons are linked together like chains. Messages are sent along the nerves to and from the brain and spinal cord. But just how does a message travel along a nerve cell? At first it was thought that nerve messages (impulses) travel along a neuron in the form of an electric current, just as messages are carried along a telephone wire. Indeed, sensitive instruments can pick up and measure tiny electric currents coming from the brain and other parts of the body. But soon it was discovered that things are not so simple.

Messages travel along nerves much more slowly than they do along a telephone wire. Scientists have learned that a dead nerve cell can still conduct electricity if you connect it to a battery. But it will not carry a nerve impulse anymore. When an electric current is passed through a nerve cell, the signal becomes weaker the farther it has to go. But the strength of a nerve impulse remains constant along its whole journey.

Scientists now believe that nerves carry messages by a kind of electrochemical reaction. This is something like the electrochemical reactions in a car battery that provide electric power for the starter and headlights. Chemical reactions in one part of the nerve fiber produce electric charges, and these charges in turn start off a chemical reaction in the next part of the fiber. In this way the impulse is carried all the way to the end of the fiber.

What happens when an impulse gets to the end of a nerve fiber? You might expect that each neuron would be hooked up to the next, and the message would simply flow along the line. But this is not the case. Although the terminal branches of one neuron are very close to the dendrites of the next, there is a tiny gap of about 25 nanometers (about a millionth of an inch or 0.000025 millimeter) between them. This gap is called a **synapse**, and it is filled with a liquid. When the nerve impulse reaches the end of the terminal branches, the electrochemical reaction comes to a stop, because it can occur only in the special substance of the nerve fiber.

Now the terminal branches produce a special chemical called a **neuro-transmitter**. Particles of this chemical drift slowly out into the liquid that fills the gap and cross it. When these particles reach the dendrites of the next neuron, they are picked up by special chemicals on the cell membrane, called receptors, and set off a reaction that starts a new impulse traveling along it.

You might imagine a nerve impulse as a fast express train, speeding along a railroad track. Suddenly it reaches a riverbank, and the tracks come to an end. The train stops, and now a ferryboat slowly carries it across to the other side. There the railroad tracks begin again, and soon the train is speeding along once more.

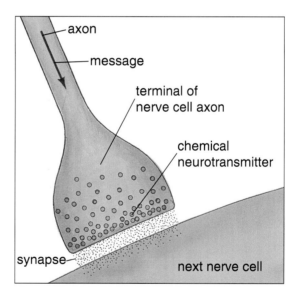

A message travels from one nerve cell to the next even though there is a gap between the cells. A chemical neurotransmitter carries the message across the gap.

We've already seen some important differences between nerves and telephone wires. Another is the fact that the same telephone wire can carry many different kinds of messages. It will carry any words you can think of, and any possible combinations of words. Telephone wires can even carry signals that can be turned into printed messages (such as a fax) or televi-

Optical fibers such as these can transmit messages in the form of pulses of light. The pulses travel much more quickly than in a telephone wire.

sion pictures at the other end. But a neuron can carry only one kind of message, and all the neurons of the body carry the same kind of impulse. How, then, can nerve impulses carry any meaningful information?

The answer lies in the way the nerves of the body are linked into a complicated network. Each neuron may have as many as 100,000 synapses connecting it to other neurons. So an impulse starting at a particular neuron could travel over many different pathways—each one conveying a different message.

For example, a special kind of nerve cell in a fingertip is linked up with a certain part of the brain. When a message is received from this neuron, it is received as a signal that something has touched the skin of the finger.

HOW FAST DO IMPULSES TRAVEL?

Electric current in a telephone wire:
   300,000,000 meters/second (186,000 miles/second)

Impulse in myelinated neuron:
   100 meters/second (about 325 feet/second)

Impulse in unmyelinated neuron:
   0.5 meter/second (about 1.5 feet/second)

Impulse across synapse:
   0.25 millimeter/second (about 0.01 inch/second)

It takes less than 1/10,000 of a second for a nerve impulse to cross over a synapse.

Messages from other types of nerve cells in the same fingertip are interpreted as signals of heat, cold, or pain. Messages sent from the brain to a muscle or organ may make it relax or contract, depending on which nerve cells carried them. The number of impulses that are carried each second also hold information, such as how strong the pain was or how much a muscle should contract. The types of neurotransmitters that carry impulses across synapses and the receptors that pick them up can determine whether an impulse will cause an action or inhibit it. Thus, the same kinds of impulses can be made to carry many different meanings.

REFLEXES

Without giving any warning, carefully snap your fingers in front of a friend's eyes. Your friend will blink. If you accidentally touch something hot, before you even feel the pain you will pull your hand away. These activities are automatic actions and are called reflexes. Some reflex actions, such as breathing, swallowing, and vomiting, are controlled by centers in the lower brain. But many reflexes, such as drawing your hand away from something painful, are controlled by the spinal cord.

The messages that set off a reflex pass through the spinal nerves along a special pathway called a **reflex arc**. The reflex arc is made up of three kinds of neurons: sensory, motor, and connector. Remember that sensory neurons carry messages to the brain or spinal cord, while motor neurons carry messages away from the brain or spinal cord. **Connector neurons** are nerve cells in the brain or spinal cord that connect two other neurons.

When you touch a hot pot, special sensitive nerve cells in the skin of your hand send out emergency messages. These messages travel along a sensory neuron to the spinal cord. There the terminal branches of the sensory neuron form synapses with the dendrites of several connector neurons. One of the connector neurons provides a connection with motor neurons running to your arm muscles. Quickly the messages flash along the motor neurons, and you pull your hand away. Meanwhile, messages are flashing along other connector neurons that lead to the brain. After the brain analyzes these messages, you are finally aware that you were touching something painfully hot. But by this time the brain is also getting messages from sense cells in parts of your arm indicating that you have already pulled your hand away from the heat.

By the time we are born, we already have many reflex arcs. Some of these disappear when they are no longer needed. Other reflex arcs become established gradually as our bodies develop. And some we can establish ourselves by consciously learning and practicing.

For example, a light touch on the cheek will cause a newborn baby to automatically turn its face toward that side and make sucking movements with its mouth. In this way, the infant can get food even before it is old enough to think about eating. A newborn baby will tightly curl its fingers around something solid that touches its hand. In primitive times, such a reflex may have helped infants to hold on while their mothers hurried through the jungle. Both of these reflexes disappear as the growing baby gains more control over its body.

Orangutan young have a strong grasping reflex just as human infants do.

A newborn baby will not blink if something comes close to its eyes. But this reflex soon appears as the baby grows. Then more and more actions are learned and become automatic. The baby learns to sit up, crawl, and walk. The toddler soon learns to eat with a spoon and fork and to put on clothes. These actions become so automatic that a child can listen to the radio or talk or even watch television while doing them.

A reflex action occurs in response to a signal, or **stimulus**. When you touch a hot pot and pull your hand away, the heat of the pot is the stimulus. But a Russian physiologist, Ivan Pavlov, discovered that sometimes a reflex action may follow a stimulus that is not directly related to it. He conducted a series of experiments on dogs. First he discovered that when a dog is shown a piece of meat, saliva soon drips from its mouth. Then Pavlov rang a bell each time he showed meat to the dog. The dog salivated each time. The next step was to ring the bell without showing the dog any meat. The dog salivated just the same. The dog had learned to associate the sound of the bell with the sight and smell of the meat, and its body acted just as though a tasty meal had been presented to it. Pavlov named this kind of reflex action a **conditioned reflex**. People can also learn by conditioned reflex.

Some conditioned reflexes can save your life. When you come to an intersection and see that the light is red, you automatically stop. Even if the light is green and you begin to cross the street, you will stop short and jump back if you suddenly see a speeding car. And the driver of a car will automatically jam on the brake if he or she sees a child dash out into the street.

BRAIN WAVES

As an impulse travels along a nerve, a tiny amount of electricity is generated. Altogether the brain only uses about as much power as a 10-watt light bulb. The electrical patterns that are produced by the brain's nerve activity are called **brain waves**.

Brain waves were first discovered in 1875 by Richard Caton, an English physiologist. Dr. Caton used metal probes (**electrodes**) that were actually inserted into the brain, but in 1929 a German doctor, Hans Berger, discovered that the brain's electricity could be detected with electrodes on the outside of the head. Today doctors can record brain waves using an **electroencephalograph (EEG)**, a machine based on Dr. Berger's discovery. To measure electrical activity in the brain, electrodes in the form of metal disks are pasted onto a patient's forehead and scalp. Wires connect the electrodes to a display screen. Electrical signals from the brain are picked up by the electrodes. Doctors can watch the brain waves on the screen, or it can be printed out on a piece of paper.

A technician uses an electroencephalograph to record a patient's brain waves.

Hans Berger noticed that there were different kinds of brain waves. When a person is awake but relaxed, brain waves occur in a regular pattern, about 8 to 13 cycles per second. Dr. Berger named these waves alpha waves.

When a person begins to think about something or is attentive, the waves become smaller and speed up to about 13 to 30 cycles per second. Dr. Berger named these beta waves.

Delta waves are large and slow (fewer than 4 cycles per second) and occur when an adult is in a deep sleep. This is also a normal brain-wave pattern for infants. Delta waves in a conscious adult can be an indication of severe brain damage or injury.

Theta waves are large and slow (4 to 8 cycles per second) and are recorded in children and at times of emotional stress in adults.

These brain wave patterns are the result of electrical activity that goes on continuously. Sensory stimulation, such as a pinprick on the skin or a light shining in a person's eyes, may trigger a burst of electrical activity that makes the brain wave pattern more complex.

Doctors can use an EEG to help in deciding whether there is a problem in a patient's brain. The patient's EEG is compared to the brain waves of a normal healthy person. The brain waves may look different when there is brain damage due to an accident, a stroke, or disease.

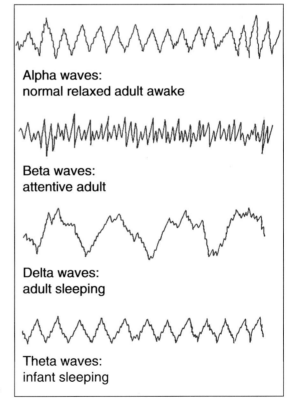

Alpha waves:
normal relaxed adult awake

Beta waves:
attentive adult

Delta waves:
adult sleeping

Theta waves:
infant sleeping

Some examples of normal brain-wave patterns

SECTION 2

THE CEREBRUM

The cerebrum contains the highest centers of the brain—centers for sensory perception, motor control, memory, association, thought, and personality. This is the part of the brain that contributes most to our "humanness." And so it is not surprising that the better developed an animal's cerebral cortex is, the more like a human it behaves. The most humanlike animals, the monkeys and apes, have the most highly developed cerebral cortex, next to that of humans.

Science fiction movies and books often show humans of the future with a large egghead with a greatly enlarged forebrain. Modern humans have far more highly developed cerebrums than our ancestors, so it is reasonable to assume that the next step in evolution would be an even greater development of this vital thinking part of the brain. As it is, the cerebrum makes up a large part of the present-day human brain—about seven-eighths of the total weight—and entirely fills the upper part of the skull.

The cerebrum is composed of a mixture of gray and white matter. The outer layer, or cerebral cortex, consists entirely of gray matter, varying from 0.06 to 0.16 inch (1.5 to 4 millimeters) thick. It is in the cortex that most of the cerebrum's activity takes place. Beneath this gray outer coat, most of the brain is white matter, but isolated masses of gray matter are scattered throughout.

The many wrinkles and furrows that mark the surface of the human cerebrum are called **convolutions**, and the human brain has far more of them than are found in any other animal. (Only monkeys, apes, and dolphins come close). Because the human cerebral cortex is convoluted, it can contain many more cells than would fit into the same space if it were smooth. You can see this by crumpling up a sheet of newspaper. From a sheet so large that you have to stretch to reach the ends, you can make a crumpled mass small enough to fit easily inside your fist. Yet the same number of letters are still printed on the paper. The raised ridges on the surface of the brain are called gyri, and the furrows between them are called sulci. The largest sulci are referred to as fissures.

A large fissure running along the middle of the brain seems to divide the cerebrum into two halves, or **hemispheres**, the left and the right. A deep cleft runs from the front to back along the middle of the cerebrum. But the left and right hemispheres of the cerebrum are not completely separated; deep inside the brain, a thick cable of nerve fibers links the two halves together. The connection, called the **corpus callosum**, contains more than 200 million nerve fibers.

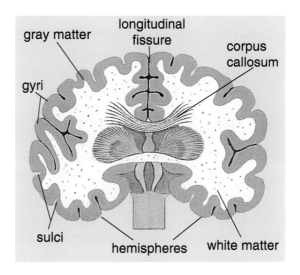

A cross section of the human brain, showing how it is divided into two hemispheres

To map out the brain, scientists divide each half, or hemisphere of the cerebrum into four lobes: the **frontal lobes** (in the front, or forehead area), the **temporal lobes** (on the sides just above the ears—the temples), the **parietal lobes** (the upper part of the head), and the **occipital lobes** (at the back of the head). Each lobe fits into a depression in the skull.

Oddly enough, the nerves connecting the cerebrum with the rest of the body cross over to the opposite side as they enter the brain. Not only are the connections reversed in this way, they are also upside down. The nerves linking the brain with the feet and the lower parts of the body have their connections near the top of the cerebral cortex. The nerves from the face and head are connected near the bottom of the cerebrum.

THE CEREBRAL CORTEX

The cerebral cortex, the "thinking brain" that makes you human, is less than 0.75 inch (6 millimeters) deep. But this thin layer is made up of 10 to 14 billion neurons. Every thought that passes through your mind and every voluntary movement you make involve some of these neurons.

Voluntary actions of all parts of the body are controlled by narrow strips of the cortex (one on each side) called the **motor strips**. This part of the brain controls muscle groups rather than individual muscles. Impulses travel down into the spinal cord and are transmitted through peripheral nerves to the correct individual muscles, causing them to contract and produce the desired movement.

Each part of the body has a corresponding spot on the motor strip on the opposite side of the brain, arranged upside down. Impulses that control the movements of the feet come from the top of the motor strips. Then, going downward, come the areas for the legs, body, hands, head and face, and mouth. The areas for the face and hands are much larger than those for any other body part. This is because the hands and face have many more things to do than the rest of the body. They have many muscles, which are very finely controlled.

Next to the motor strip, to the rear of a large fissure that runs down the side of each cerebral hemisphere, lies a **sensory strip**. Touch, pressure, and other skin sensations from various parts of the body are carried by nerves to this part of the cortex. Like the motor strips, each sensory strip has an upside-down arrangement (feet sensations at the top) and corresponds to the opposite side of the body. Here, too, the hands and face have a far larger share than you might guess from their size.

The specialized sense organs of the body—the eyes, ears, nose, and taste buds—have their own control centers on the cortex. You may "see stars" after being hit on the head because of a blow to the visual area, in

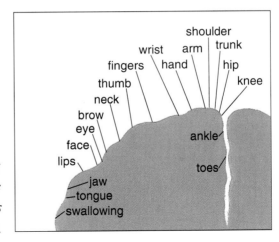

Nerve impulses controlling muscles in various parts of the body come from the motor strips of the cerebral cortex.

the occipital lobes. Normally your eyes gather information on light, color, and the shapes of things, but all these data don't make pictures until they are analyzed in the visual cortex. There is also an auditory area (in the temporal lobes) for hearing. Hearing involves more than receiving vibrations in the ear. The vibrations stimulate impulses that are sent to the auditory area of the cortex and are interpreted into sounds. The cortex also contains areas for taste and smell, and association areas are concerned with learning and the memory of things seen and heard.

Several different parts of the cortex are associated with speech. The motor speech area in the motor cortex is involved in the actual physical movements that form speech. A speech area in another part of the cortex is concerned with the choice of thoughts to be expressed; another area deals with the choice of words. Still another is involved in word formation.

Damage to different parts of the brain can produce various kinds of speech problems, because different language activities are controlled by different parts of the brain. Damage in one area might make a person unable to speak, or unable to speak intelligibly. Damage to other parts of the brain can cause a person to be unable to write, unable to understand spoken words, or unable to understand written words. Such conditions are common after a person suffers a **stroke**. Stroke victims' minds may be sharp and logical, and they may know exactly what they want to say, but when they open their mouths only nonsense syllables come out. Or they may be able to hear people speaking perfectly well but be unable to make any sense out of what they are hearing.

RIGHT BRAIN, LEFT BRAIN

The brain's crisscross wiring means that movements of the left side of the body are controlled by the right side of the brain, and vice versa. But in many brain functions, the two hemispheres of the brain do not play equal roles. One side becomes more developed than the other for particular activities, such as speech or drawing pictures. One hemisphere is usually better developed than the other in manipulating the parts of the body, too. That is the reason you are probably better at doing things with one hand than with the other, even if you have tried to practice with both. If you are right-handed, it is actually the left hemisphere of your brain that is better developed; if you are left-handed, your right hemisphere is dominant. Handedness is often established by the age of three, and about nine out of ten people are right-handed.

Testing to see which side of the brain is dominant

Usually the dominant hemisphere controls a person's ability to speak, as well as some other important functions. If a stroke or an accident damages these control centers in the dominant hemisphere, a person will lose the ability to speak at first. But gradually the other hemisphere can learn to take over the job of control to some degree.

Scientists have learned about the functions of different parts of the brain by observing animal and human brains. Surprisingly, the brain is not sensitive to pain. So a surgeon can cut a tumor out of a patient's brain while the patient is wide awake. During surgery, the doctor may stimulate specific places on the cortex with small wire electrodes that deliver a tiny electric current. Observing what happens helps to determine which brain functions have been damaged and also provides information about brain functions. This is one way that "brain maps" have been worked out.

A particular region of the cortex may cause the patient to clench a fist suddenly, or kick out a foot. When a different area is stimulated, the patient may suddenly see colors, smell flowers, or hear the voice of a childhood friend.

Doctors have also learned a lot by studying patients with epilepsy, a disease in which the brain's electrical activity becomes erratic, causing seizures or unconsciousness. In rare cases, epilepsy has been treated by surgically cutting the connections between the hemispheres of the brain, producing a split-brain. A split-brain person literally has two independent brains in one skull. Normally there are no obvious outward signs of this extraordinary situation. Both hemispheres of the brain receive sensory information and are usually well enough informed. But in experiments, the two sides of the brain can be tested independently.

In some studies, different pictures are flashed on the two sides of a split screen. Split-brain volunteers have helped scientists discover that the left brain is the verbal half, which reads, writes, and speaks fluently and does difficult arithmetic. The right brain can read common words, do simple arithmetic, and understand simple verbal instructions. The right brain has a keener sense of shape, form, and texture, as well as a flair for musical rhythm and melody, intuition, creativity, and a sense of humor. (These generalizations are true for most right-handers, but left-handers may have their verbal and logical centers in the right brain.) Because the sides of the brain can no longer exchange information, a split-brain person feeling in a bag of objects with the left hand cannot say the name of the object that was grasped—the left brain, in charge of speech, did not receive any information from the left hand. (Remember that sensory information from various parts of the body is relayed to the opposite side of the brain.)

THE CEREBELLUM

Close your eyes and stretch your hands out to the sides. Now slowly bring them forward until you touch your fingertips together. You can do this very easily. But if you had had an accident that damaged your cerebellum, you would not have been able to perform this simple task. Your hands would jerk about, no matter how hard you tried to control them. You would also be unable to catch and throw a ball, to run and jump, or even to walk without staggering and falling.

The cerebral cortex plays an important role in controlling the muscle contractions that move body parts. But the part of the brain that makes sure that your muscles work together is the cerebellum. It helps to coordinate body movements and makes sure that each muscle contracts not too much or too little, but just enough to carry out the cerebrum's instructions. When you throw a ball to a friend, your hands, legs, eyes, and many other parts of your body must work together. The cerebellum also helps your body keep its balance and manages the continual adjustments needed for posture.

The cerebellum is found behind the brain stem, nestled under the overhang of the cerebrum. Cerebellum means "little brain," and, indeed, this portion of the hindbrain looks very much like a smaller version of the cerebrum. Like the cerebrum, it has a convoluted surface, is made up of a mixture of gray and white matter, and is divided into two hemispheres. Very large neurons in the cerebellar cortex, called Purkinje cells, form synapses with as many as 200,000 nerve fibers.

The cerebellum receives a continual flow of messages telling it where the various body parts are, whether they are moving, and, if so, in what direction and how fast. It also receives information from the motor region

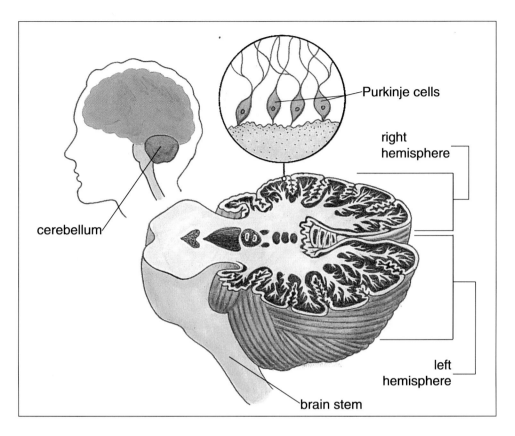

A cross section of the cerebellum and its location in the brain

of the cerebral cortex. The cerebellum compares the movements the cortex has ordered with what the body is actually doing and sends messages to the muscles to make adjustments, if necessary. The correction occurs much faster than it would if you had to think consciously about each movement.

As you practice a physical activity—whether it is drawing, riding a bicycle, or pitching a baseball—you gradually get better at it. That is because your cerebellum is getting more accurate in its corrections.

THE PRIMITIVE BRAIN

How long can you hold your breath? Probably not for even a minute. Suddenly, whether you want to or not, you are forced to breathe again. As you held your breath, trillions of cells in the body gave off carbon dioxide into your blood. This gas normally passes into the lungs and is breathed out. But since you were not breathing, carbon dioxide built up in the blood and stimulated sensitive cells in some of the blood vessels. These in turn sent messages to the breathing center in the medulla, and this center sent out messages to the muscles around your lungs, forcing you to breathe. In addition to the breathing center, the medulla oblongata also houses important control centers for the heartbeat and the widening and narrowing of the blood vessels.

The medulla also contains separate centers that control swallowing and vomiting. If you drink a little water and begin to swallow it, you will find that once you have started to swallow you cannot stop. It becomes automatic. The vomiting mechanism can be very important, too, for that is how the body gets rid of poisons that are accidentally eaten. Rats do not have a vomiting center; that is why certain rat poisons kill rats very effectively but do not harm other animals that happen to eat the poisons—the other animals simply vomit them up. The medulla is also involved with coughing, sneezing, and hiccuping. The **vestibular complex**, found in the medulla as well, is important for maintaining balance.

The midbrain (mesencephalon) is a small region connecting the forebrain with the hindbrain. In lower animals such as fish and reptiles, the midbrain is the major region for receiving and processing information from the organs of sight and hearing. In humans, these functions have mostly been taken over by the cerebral cortex, and the midbrain controls optic reflexes such as blinking, the opening of the pupil, and the focusing of the eye lens. Scientists once believed that the adjustment of the opening of the pupils was a simple reflex, dependent on the amount of light striking the eyes. However, researchers observing volunteers' reactions to pictures found that the pupils tend to widen when people are looking at things they find interesting. Another center in the midbrain controls the auditory reflexes, adjusting the ears to the amount of sound coming in.

Running up through the brain stem, from the medulla and pons into the thalamus and hypothalamus, is a cone-shaped network of neurons called the reticular formation. (*Reticulum* means "net.") It houses the **reticular activating system**, or **RAS**. This is a sort of central clearinghouse for the flood of sense information that comes into the brain. The RAS determines which of the many bits of information are important enough—or novel enough—to report to the higher brain.

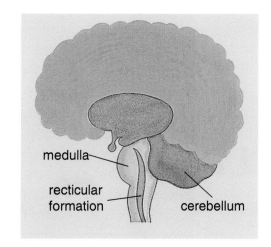

Have you ever noticed that you can forget about some distraction, such as the noise of a pneumatic drill in the street outside, if you are very interested in something else—reading a good book, for example, or playing an exciting game? Your RAS is blocking the messages from your ears, permitting your conscious brain to concentrate on more interesting and important things. Without the RAS to block out some of the incoming information, the cerebrum would be swamped; it could not concentrate on anything in particular, and you would be thoroughly confused.

Minor aches and pains often seem unbearable at night, and small noises like the ticking of a clock seem more distracting then, because the sense organs are not sending in as much other information. With less competition, the RAS sends these signals through to the higher brain.

THE THALAMUS AND THE HYPOTHALAMUS

At the base of the cerebral hemispheres, buried deep within the brain, is the **diencephalon**, or 'tweenbrain. It contains several important structures including the thalamus, the hypothalamus, and the **pineal gland**.

The thalamus is like a complex telephone switching center. This pair of egg-shaped masses of gray matter is the central relay station of the brain, involved in a complex network of interconnections between the cerebral cortex and the spinal cord. Messages from all the sense receptors, except those of smell, are filtered through the thalamus, where these messages are analyzed before they are relayed to the proper areas of the cortex. The nerve connections run both ways. Impulses from the motor cortex are relayed through the thalamus to the spinal cord. The thalamus is involved in many reflexes, especially visual and auditory ones.

In lower animals the thalamus provides for awareness of the surroundings. In people this part of the brain provides only a rough awareness. Finer details are filled in by the cerebral cortex.

The hypothalamus is about the size of a pea and weighs only 1/300 of the total mass of the brain, but it is an important link in the body's physical and emotional life. The hypothalamus is a mass of gray matter below each thalamus. (Its name means "under the thalamus.") Sensory nerve fibers bring messages to the hypothalamus from the cerebral cortex, the thalamus, and the brain stem. Motor fibers link the hypothalamus to the thalamus, brain stem, and spinal cord. The hypothalamus acts as a central monitoring and control station in many body activities.

It is the hypothalamus that helps to keep our body temperature at about 98.6°F (37°C), no matter how hot or cold it is outside. Sometimes when you are ill, your body temperature goes up and you have a fever. That is because billions of bacteria or viruses swarm in your blood when you are

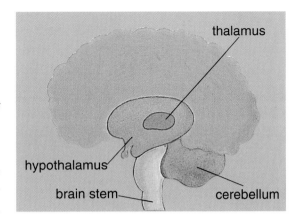

The hypothalamus is about the size of a pea and is located deep within the brain. Although small, it plays a large role in controlling our emotions.

ill and release poisons into your bloodstream. These poisons may upset the temperature-regulating centers in the hypothalamus. The hypothalamus is also involved in regulating such body activities as water metabolism, maintenance of blood sugar level, and reproductive cycles.

The control centers that work in people to regulate food intake are also located in the hypothalamus. There is a hunger center that makes us hungry, and a satiety center that tells us we're full. A thirst center helps regulate the water balance in the body by producing feelings of thirst when water reserves are low. One part of the hypothalamus causes us to be alert and excited, and a sleep center produces sleepiness. A number of centers associated with emotional responses have been found in the hypothalamus, both in animals and humans. There is an anger center, a fear center, a pain center, and a pleasure center.

The hypothalamus also produces hormonelike chemicals that control the work of the **pituitary gland**. The pituitary is often called the "master gland" of the endocrine system, since its secretions control and regulate the activity of the other **endocrine glands**.

In a developing embryo, the pineal gland starts out as a third eye. Before it is completely formed, it starts to degenerate. The remains of the structure, buried deep in the brain, form a small oval mass of nerve cells in part of the thalamus. The pineal gland is believed to be the body's biological clock, which keeps body rhythms in sync with the cycles of day and night.

SLEEP

Have you ever tried to stay up very late? Once you are past your regular bedtime, you find yourself growing drowsier and drowsier. If you tried very hard, you might be able to stay up all night or even longer, especially if you had something very interesting to do. But eventually you would fall asleep in spite of yourself—perhaps while you were sitting in a chair or even standing up! The sleep center in your hypothalamus has taken over.

In a number of laboratories, scientists are staying up at night to watch other people sleeping. We spend about a third of our lives asleep, and these scientists are eager to find out more about what happens during sleep and how important it is in our lives. They use various electrical instruments that record the heartbeat and the electrical waves from the brain. They wake people up to find out if they are dreaming, and they watch the sleepers' every movement.

In such studies, researchers found that people normally have a regular pattern of sleeping. At first the sleep is shallow, a sort of floating, day-

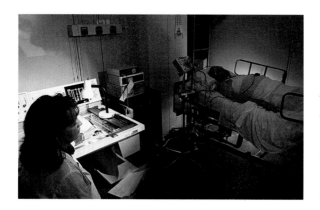

A technician monitors a sleeping patient to learn more about brain activity. Sleep restores energy to the body, particularly to the brain and nervous system.

dreaming state, but gradually the person falls more deeply asleep. In this second stage of sleep the EEG shows a typical pattern of "sleep spindles." The sleeper's heartbeat and breathing gradually slow and body temperature falls as sleep passes into the deep third stage. A person might sleepwalk or talk during this stage and have no memory of it later. Bed-wetting also occurs during deep sleep. The brain waves recorded in this stage are very slow and regular delta waves. But then they speed up, almost as though the sleeper were awakening. Instead, a dream is beginning. The sleeper's eyes move rapidly back and forth under their closed eyelids, as though watching the action of the dream. This dreaming stage has been named **REM sleep**, for the *r*apid *e*ye *m*ovements. A sleeper awakened at this stage would recall a dream in vivid detail. After a while, the rapid eye movements stop and the sleep deepens again.

The cycles of deep sleep and dreaming sleep repeat again and again through the night, every 90 minutes or so. In the first half of the night, the periods of slow-wave delta sleep are very deep. But later the sleep becomes lighter, and dreams are longer and more detailed. Both types of sleep seem to be necessary. If people are awakened and prevented from sleeping deeply or from dreaming, they begin to get very irritable and behave peculiarly. A person who is not allowed to sleep at all may even start to have hallucinations—seeing and hearing things that are not there.

Scientists have discovered a lot about sleep and dreams. But they still are not sure exactly why we sleep and dream. Some scientists think that sleep allows the body to rebuild its reserves of chemicals that have been used up in the brain and repair damaged cells. Hormones that stimulate growth and repair are secreted during sleep. Dreams seem to help the brain to sort out the experiences of the day, work out problems, and put memories in order.

How much sleep do you need? Some people seem able to get along with just a few hours of sleep a night, perhaps with some brief naps during the day, but most adults need at least seven or eight hours a night. Children need even more sleep to stay healthy. (Remember that growth occurs during sleep.) Researchers say that there are so many pressures and things to do in our modern world that many people do not get enough sleep—and as a result, they are less efficient and more likely to have accidents than they would be if they were well rested.

THE AUTONOMIC NERVOUS SYSTEM

Unless something goes wrong, we usually have little conscious awareness of what goes on inside our bodies. The heart and blood vessels, the lungs, the organs of the digestive system—all of these body parts must be as finely coordinated as the musicians of a symphony orchestra. This is accomplished because many signals are sent to the central nervous system through the peripheral nervous system to report on the condition of the body. Only a small number of these reports are ever brought to our conscious attention. Appropriate actions are usually taken automatically and independently of the conscious brain. The blood vessel diameters are continually being adjusted to direct the blood flow to the most needy areas. The heart and respiration rates are speeded up or slowed down as needed, as are the movements and secretions of the stomach and intestines and a number of other body processes.

The nerves involved in the control and coordination of these body activities form a part of the peripheral nervous system called the autonomic nervous system. The term *autonomic* literally means self-controlled and independent of outside influences. But the nerves of the autonomic nervous system really work closely with many other parts of the nervous system, especially the hypothalamus.

Although the workings of the autonomic nervous system are rarely brought to our conscious attention, they are closely linked with our emotional state. The common phrases "broke out in a cold sweat," "feeling warm and contented," "a sinking feeling in the stomach," and many others are reflections of effects produced by the autonomic nervous system that accompany particular emotional states.

An important function of the autonomic system is concerned with keeping the body systems running smoothly, day in and day out. This job is handled by a network of autonomic nerves called the **parasympathetic nervous system**. But sometimes emergencies arise. These situations are handled by the **sympathetic nervous system**.

Sympathetic nerves go from the spinal cord to various parts of the body. They are made up only of motor nerve fibers. Some of them go to the muscles around the body hairs; messages from sympathetic neurons to these muscles cause them to contract and make the hairs stand up. This effect makes a furry animal look bigger; in humans, whose body hair is very sparse, it just produces goose bumps. Other sympathetic nerves make the blood vessels get narrower. This helps to protect us in emergencies, by reducing bleeding if we are cut.

Sympathetic nerves make the heart beat faster and make breathing easier by widening the air passages. Still other sympathetic nerves slow down the work of the stomach and intestines and direct the blood supply away from these organs to the heart and muscles. This allows the body to concentrate its energies to be ready to either run from danger or stand and fight. This is called the flight or fight response. Messages from the sympathetic nervous system also stimulate one of the glands of the body to pour out a hormone called **adrenaline** into the bloodstream. Adrenaline has the same kind of effect as the sympathetic nerves and works to make their action even stronger.

Like the nerves of the sympathetic nervous system, those of the parasympathetic nervous system are also all motor nerves. They go to all the same parts of the body, but their actions are exactly the opposite. Parasympathetic nerves slow down the heartbeat and widen the arteries just below the skin. They speed up the work of the stomach and intestines and narrow air passages. In other words, the sympathetic nervous system stirs us up, while the parasympathetic system calms us down. It helps to keep our bodies running smoothly under normal conditions, when we do not have to get ready for an emergency.

For a long time it was believed that we had no voluntary control over the autonomic nervous system. It was even called the "involuntary nervous system." However, many religious mystics have long claimed to be able to control their heartbeat and respiration rate at will. It was not until the late

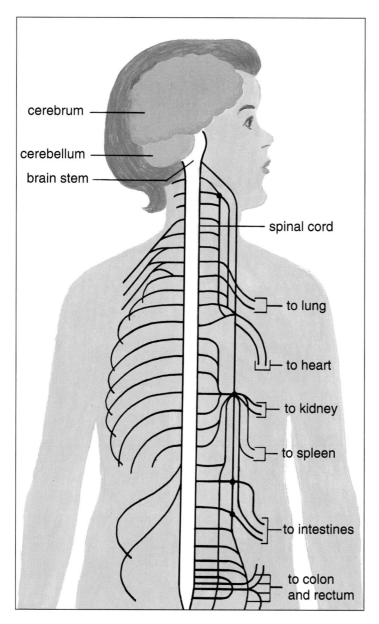

cerebrum

cerebellum

brain stem

spinal cord

to lung

to heart

to kidney

to spleen

to intestines

to colon
and rectum

The nerves of the sympathetic and parasympathetic nervous systems go to the same parts of the body, but the two systems have different effects. The sympathetic nervous system causes changes in the body to handle emergencies. The parasympathetic nervous system keeps the body running smoothly under normal conditions.

1950s that scientists began to investigate these claims. Researchers have found that yogis in India, for example, have remarkable control over their bodies. One yogi was placed in an airtight box, with electrodes attached to his body to show his heart rate, breathing rate, body temperature, and brain waves. Inside the box, the yogi's breathing slowed, and he took in only one-quarter of the amount of oxygen scientists had assumed was the minimum amount needed to stay alive. Several hours later the box was opened, and the yogi was alive and well!

Scientists have also found that dogs and rats can be trained to control their heart rate, blood pressure, and many other autonomic body functions. Rats have even been trained to dilate the blood vessels in one ear and not the other, producing a one-sided "blush"!

Biofeedback has been used by doctors to help patients reduce migraine headaches or slow down their heart rate or blood pressure. In this procedure, the patient slowly learns how to control these bodily functions by receiving feedback signals, such as a light or a bell that indicates when the desired heart rate or blood pressure reading has been reached. Then it becomes easier and easier as the person learns how to produce that change.

HORMONES

Two communication systems help to keep the body running smoothly. Some messages are sent along the nerves as nerve impulses; others are carried by special chemicals called hormones. Most of the hormones are proteins, but some are fatlike substances called **steroids**. Most hormones are produced in structures called endocrine glands and are released (or secreted) into the bloodstream, which carries them to various parts of the body. The hypothalamus helps to control hormone secretion.

A nerve impulse travels from the brain to a part of the body in a tiny fraction of a second. Hormones cannot travel as fast, but their effects last longer. These two messenger systems often work together—the nervous system starts off changes in body conditions and operates when quick action is needed, while hormones promote and maintain the effects over the long-term.

Hormones are involved in many of our daily activities. They help children to grow, and help people of all ages to digest food. Hormones help to keep the amounts of water, sugar, and salts at the right levels in the body.

The pituitary gland, nestled beneath the brain, is often called the "master gland." It is only the size of a pea, but it makes many different types of hormones and controls many other endocrine glands. One of the pituitary hormones helps to control growth. If too much is produced, a person can become a giant; too little, and the person may become a dwarf.

The adrenal glands, which lie on top of the kidneys, make hormones that help us to deal with shock and stress. They also make the hormone adrenaline, which gives us a burst of energy when we are angry, nervous, or frightened. Adrenaline's effects are very similar to those of the sympathetic nervous system.

The pancreas controls the use of glucose, the body's energy source. One of its hormones, insulin, causes glucose to be removed from the blood and stored in the liver in the form of a starch. Another pancreatic hormone, glucagon, has the opposite effect, prompting the release of glucose from the liver into the blood when body cells need more energy.

The thyroid gland, found in the neck, controls the rate at which the body uses up the energy that we get from food. The parathyroid gland, four small structures embedded inside the thyroid, helps to control the level of calcium in the blood. The thymus gland helps the body fight germs.

The ovaries in females and testes in males produce hormones that help people to become sexually mature and have children.

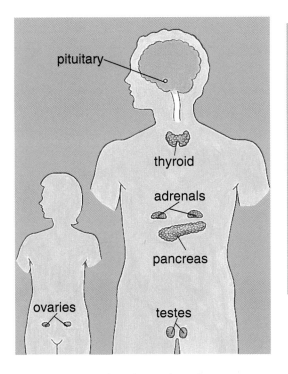

Endocrine glands produce hormones, which are the body's chemical messengers.

DO STEROIDS PUMP UP MUSCLES?

The male sex hormone, testosterone, is a steroid that helps boys to mature sexually. Part of its effect is to promote the formation of large, strong muscles. Some athletes take synthetic steroids with testosteronelike effects in an attempt to develop their bodies faster and become more aggressive. This kind of drug use is illegal, and synthetic steroids have some unpleasant and even dangerous side effects. The best way to develop muscles is through regular exercise.

THE LIMBIC SYSTEM

A horseshoe-shaped area of the brain, called the **limbic system**, is mainly concerned with our emotions. This "emotional brain" includes many different parts of the brain, such as portions of the cerebral cortex, the thalamus, the hypothalamus, and the reticular formation in the brainstem.

A key structure of the limbic system is the **amygdala**, two knobby masses of tissue found just above the pituitary gland. (Its name comes from a word meaning "almond.") The amygdala has connections to all parts of the limbic system and also to the parts of the cerebral cortex involved in sight and sound. Experiences that arouse emotions are sent through the amygdala to other parts of the brain, especially the hypothalamus.

Another important part of the limbic system is the **hippocampus**, a pair of structures shaped like sea horses (which is what their name means

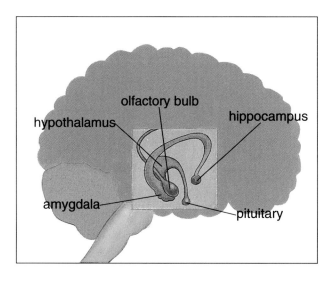

The amygdala and hippocampus are two important parts of the limbic system. This drawing shows their location in the brain.

in Greek) or bean pods. The hippocampus seems to be essential for forming long-term memories. People who have had their hippocampus damaged or removed can remember everything that happened before the operation, but they cannot learn or remember any new information for more than a few minutes.

The limbic system colors our thoughts with emotions. This part of the brain provides a set of instincts to help animals cope with the world around them. In humans, sometimes the emotional feelings of the limbic system clash with the rational decisions made in the higher brain. Often we can deny or bury our feelings. For example, an "instinctive" fear of high places or of large animals can gradually be overcome. But sometimes the struggle between the limbic system and the higher brain can cause conflicts that are finally expressed in physical problems such as ulcers, skin rashes, and chronic fatigue.

MEMORY

Wouldn't it be great if you had a photographic **memory**? Then you'd be able to remember everything in your textbooks after just a single quick reading. Some people do have such a memory. They can visualize in their minds a sort of photograph of things that they have seen or read. In fact, some people are able to remember nearly every detail of everything they have ever experienced.

WHAT A MEMORY!

In 1967 a man in Turkey took six hours to recite from memory 6,666 verses of the Koran, the holy book of the Islamic religion. In 1974 someone topped that by reciting 16,000 pages of Buddhist texts!

Most of us remember far less easily and much more selectively. Our brains are constantly receiving a blizzard of information. We remember only a few of the most important details. Even so, our brains record more information than we usually realize. Under hypnosis, people have been able to recite intricate details that they did not consciously think they remembered. But memories are not always reliable—often we unconsciously change or even make up details that are added to our "real" memories. It is difficult to distinguish between false memories and long-buried memories of actual events that resurface years later.

Many scientists are studying memory and learning, and they have come up with theories that are still controversial. But it is generally accepted that there seem to be two basic kinds of memory: short-term memory and long-term memory. Short-term memory stores things that have happened within the last few minutes. Long-term memory is much longer lasting. Childhood memories may be quite vividly remembered in old age.

Let's say you look up a telephone number and then turn away to make the call. You will probably remember the phone number long enough to dial it, but if you get a wrong number, by the time you have apologized to the person on the line, hung up, and begun to redial, you will probably find you have to look up the number all over again.

Fixing a new bit of information in your long-term memory usually involves motivation, repetition, and association. You are motivated by a particular interest or pleasure, the hope of a reward, or the fear of punishment. The more times you use a new word or fact (repetition), the more fixed it becomes in your long-term memory. And memory formation is aided by associating or cross-referencing new information to things you already know. Mnemonics are handy association devices for remembering things. You probably know some mnemonics, like "i before e except after c." You can also make your own. Going to the store, for instance, you might use the word *cat* to remember to buy cookies, apples, and tea.

There is some evidence that pictures and words are stored differently in the brain. Visual images can be remembered and recognized directly, while words have to be decoded into their meanings and associations.

Scientists are not totally sure what happens in the brain during learning or how memories are stored and retrieved. Currently it is believed that memories consist of specific pathways of linked-up neurons. Special chemicals, produced in the neurons as the memory is being formed, may act as signposts, sending the nerve impulses along the right path. It is also thought that each memory is stored in many different parts of the brain. All of the parts together create a sharp, vivid memory. But when some of the storage places are lost, the memory becomes fuzzier.

INTELLIGENCE AND LEARNING

To solve the daily problems of living, most animals rely on instinct instead of learning and memory. An instinct is an ability or a behavior that an animal never had to learn—it is built right into the nervous system. For example, when a bird takes off into the air for the first time, it already knows how to fly. It just has to practice a little to get better and better.

Human babies are born with some instincts, too, but not as many as most other animals. Most of these instinctive behaviors disappear as the child gets older and starts to learn and remember how to do things.

Some of the early studies on animals revealed that they tend to learn things by a process of trial and error. In other words, an animal tries out an action. If this action happens to solve the problem, the animal may remember this the next time it faces the same problem and try the same action again. For example, if a rat pushes a lever and a food pellet pops out of a hole, it may push the lever again. If the rat scratches at the hole where the

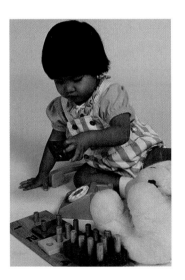

food pellet comes out and nothing happens, eventually it learns that this action does not bring food. Gradually it learns which actions have good results and which do not, and it will solve the problem every time.

Trial and error is the way a child learns to stack blocks and to open a jar. But some scientists felt that this theory could not explain all of human learning. A human being has a much more developed cerebral cortex than a rat or a dog and is capable of much more complicated actions. A rat or a dog could never learn to drive a car or write a poem.

Chimpanzees' brains are much closer to those of humans, and studies of their learning behavior led to a new theory. In one experiment, a researcher hung a banana outside a chimpanzee's cage, just out of reach. A cat, trying to get a piece of meat in a similar situation, probably would have tried to pull at the meat with its paw. Then it might have meowed and rubbed and scratched against the bars of its cage. Using these trial and error methods, the cat would never have been able to solve the problem. But the chimpanzee simply looked up at the banana and then down at a long stick lying on the floor of the cage. Then the chimpanzee picked up the stick and knocked the banana into the cage.

Scientists call this type of problem solving insight learning. The animal (or person) seems to "see into" the problem and figure out what is needed to solve it. Bits of past experience are put together to find the answer without actually physically trying out anything.

Theories such as trial and error and insight learning have provided some good descriptions of the ways in which we learn. They have been used to help change methods of teaching in schools. But now scientists are trying to go deeper into the actual processes of learning and remembering, using new tools to study how the brain works.

Memory and the ability to learn are part of a complex set of abilities that we call **intelligence**. Other aspects of intelligence are the ability to solve problems, the ability to anticipate the results of actions, and various forms of creativity. Some people seem to have more of a natural ability to learn, remember, and solve problems than others. But many experts believe that the "intelligence tests" used today do not really measure mental ability; instead, they are only gauges of what an individual has learned.

ARTIFICIAL INTELLIGENCE

Which is "smarter"—a human brain or a computer? Computers can perform some tasks, such as arithmetic problems, much faster than any human. But a human brain can do many more things than any computer that has been invented.

Computer scientists hope someday to create artificial intelligence—a computer that will learn from each new experience to help it perform better and better, just as a human brain does. Actually, researchers in Japan plan to develop an artificial brain by 2001. It will have more than 1 billion artificial neurons in a network inside a huge parallel computer. In effect, the network will build itself as it gathers data and needs more and more neurons to handle the load.

SECTION 3

THE NERVOUS SYSTEM AND MOVEMENT

The brain works closely with the muscles and skeleton as a combined neuromusculoskeletal system, to allow us to move. Special sensory organs called **proprioceptors** are spread throughout skeletal muscles, tendons, joints, and in the inner ear to keep the brain aware of body movements and the position of the limbs. In our muscles, proprioceptors called **muscle spindles** send messages to the brain when the muscle fibers stretch. This lets the brain know how contracted a muscle is. Muscles that perform very fine movements have more muscle spindles. Visual messages from the eyes and impulses from the skin senses also provide important information for coordinating muscular movements. Movements are produced by messages carried from the brain or spinal cord to the muscles over motor nerves.

Muscles are made up of long but very thin cells called muscle fibers. Each individual muscle fiber is capable of contracting when stimulated by the nervous system. The more muscle fibers that are stimulated, the more the whole muscle contracts. In this way many different movements are possible.

The branching motor nerves end in tiny buttonlike nerve endings called **motor end plates**. Each of these fits into a hollow on the surface of a muscle fiber. The junction between the nerve ending and the muscular fiber is called a **neuromuscular junction**, and it is very similar to a synapse between two neurons. A motor neuron and the muscle fibers it controls are called a **motor unit**.

When a child is first born there are several motor neurons that join each muscle fiber. As we grow and become better able to control our muscles, fewer connections are needed. Eventually there is only one motor neuron for a whole group of muscle fibers. A single message causes all the fibers in the group to contract.

There are an average of 150 muscle fibers in each motor unit in our bodies. The motor neurons that bring messages to muscles in the hand control much smaller groups of muscle fibers. That way the muscles are able to perform delicate and coordinated activities, such as threading a needle. There are as few as three muscle fibers in a motor unit in the tiny muscles of the eye. The muscles in the legs are large and strong. The motor neurons there control larger groups of muscle fibers, because delicate movements are not required. There may be 1,000 or more muscle fibers in each motor unit in the slow-moving calf muscle.

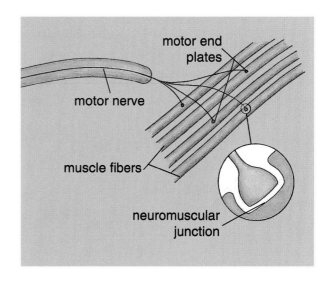

One motor neuron and the muscle fibers it controls are called a motor unit. Each motor neuron controls a specific number of muscle fibers.

When the brain sends electrical signals along the nerve fibers to the muscles, the chemical balance inside the muscle cells is changed, causing the muscle fiber to tighten or contract. The messages tell the muscles when, how much, and how long to contract.

For every movement that we make, the brain must arrange for the proper muscles to contract in the correct timing with the action of other muscles. The neuromusculoskeletal system is amazingly organized and helps us to perform complicated tasks. Even simple tasks require a lot of coordinating. Walking uses more than 100 muscles!

Standing or sitting also requires a highly coordinated use of skeletal muscles, even though it may not seem like you are moving. Muscles in your neck, back, and legs work together to help you keep your balance and posture without having to think about it. Proprioceptors in the muscles provide constant feedback to the brain, so that it can keep the muscles contracted just the right amount to keep you from toppling over.

SIGHT

A dog "sees" the world mainly in the form of a rich variety of smells. A bat can accurately locate a mosquito in flight by analyzing the ultrasonic echoes that bounce off the tiny insect. But we humans rely mainly on our sense of sight to give us information about the world. The eyes are our organs of sight, but they are only a part of the vision story. Much of the action takes place inside the brain, and that is where images are given their meaning.

When we look at an object, rays of light are reflected off it and enter our eyes. The lens of each eye focuses the rays so that they meet at the back of the eye and form an upside-down picture of what we are looking at. This area is called the **retina**. The 130 million cells that make up the retina are sensitive to light. The retinal cells send messages to the brain along the optic nerves. When the visual cortex, in the occipital lobes of the brain, receives the messages, it turns the image the right way up so that we can see properly.

Messages from the eyes are sent not only to the visual cortex but also to various parts of the primitive brain: to the hypothalamus, where they help to set the body "clocks" that control various daily cycles; to the midbrain structures that control the pupil reflexes and some of the eye movements; and to the thalamus, which relays messages up to the cortex and down into the brain stem. The optic nerve fibers cross as they pass into the brain, but their arrangement is a little different from the crisscross pattern typical of the rest of the body. The nerve fibers from the right side of each eye go to the visual cortex in the right hemisphere, and the nerve fibers from the left side of each eye end in the visual cortex of the left hemisphere. So both halves of the brain receive information from both eyes. But the right hemisphere is informed directly only about the right half of the picture, while the left hemisphere "sees" the left half.

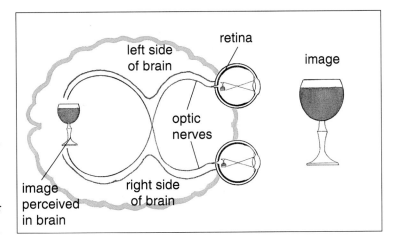

The paths of the optic nerves. This shows how an image is perceived by the eyes and then is interpreted by the brain.

If you were a dog, the world would look like a black-and-white movie to you. But humans, birds, and some other animals have color vision. There are two types of sensitive cells in the retina, rods and cones. The rods (about 90 percent of the sensitive cells) can pick up reflected light rays even when it is rather dim; they provide the black-and-white vision that allows us to distinguish shapes. Cones come in three varieties, sensitive to red, blue, or green. The messages of all these sensory cells are combined in the visual cortex to produce full-color pictures.

Our two eyes look at the world from slightly different positions, so the pictures they see are almost—but not quite—identical. The brain constantly compares the two pictures and uses the information to see a three-dimensional image. If you look at a distant scene with only one eye, things will seem flat, like a two-dimensional picture in a book. Our two-eyed, 3-D view of the world is called binocular vision.

If you watch someone reading a book, you will notice that the person's eyes are moving constantly, in tiny, jerky jumps across the page. Even when you are staring at something, your eyes still make tiny movements as they gather additional bits of information then return to the object of your gaze. The movements are so fast that you are not aware of them. Your brain automatically ignores the blurry images that the eyes send when they are moving. Your brain works in a similar way when you watch a movie or TV show. While you see a smoothly moving picture, the screen is actually showing a series of single images too fast for you to notice the gaps between them.

HEARING AND BALANCE

Your ears are actually double-duty sense organs. First of all, they gather sound information, which is transformed in the brain into the sense of hearing.

The outer ears act as sound funnels, directing sound waves into the ear canal. Our human ears are not very effective sound funnels, compared to those of many animals. A dog or a horse can prick up its ears and turn them toward sounds like an antenna.

After entering the outer ear canal, sound waves hit the eardrum. This is a tight membrane, stretched across the opening into the inner ear. Sound waves beat against the eardrum like a stick on a drum, making it vibrate. Three tiny bones (the smallest bones in the body) pass the sound vibrations along into the inner ear, where they enter the **cochlea**, a fluid-filled tube that is coiled like a snail shell. Inside the cochlea are more than 20,000 tiny hairlike fibers, which can vibrate like the reeds of a harmonica. As sound waves are transmitted through the cochlea, the vibrations of these fibers cause tiny hair cells to bend back and forth, changing the sound into signals that can be carried by nerves to the brain.

The nerve fibers leading from the cochlea enter the medulla. From there the nerve pathways branch off to various parts of the brain. Most of the fibers leading into the cerebral cortex cross over to the other side of the brain, but some stay in the hemisphere on the same

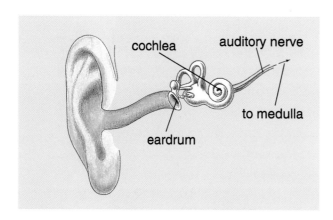

The main structures of the ear

side as the ear. Sound messages are also carried to crude sound perception centers in the midbrain and into the reticular activating system of the brain stem. When a sudden loud noise makes your body give a startled jerk, these lower brain centers are operating. Prolonged exposure to very loud noises—such as a jet engine or an amplified rock band—can destroy some of the delicate hair cells in the cochlea and lead to deafness.

The auditory cortex, in the temporal lobes at the sides of the brain, makes sense out of the sound messages delivered from the ears. These hearing centers can figure out whether sounds are high or low pitched, depending on which hair cells in the cochlea are sending signals. The ability to learn and recognize sound patterns is found in the auditory cortex, too. Your brain can determine the direction from which a sound is coming by comparing the messages from the two ears. It can distinguish the tones of music and the sounds of speech. Specialized speech areas on the cortex help in interpreting speech sounds.

But hearing is only one of the ear's sensory functions. The inner ear is also involved in our sense of balance. Small fluid-filled sacs lined with hair cells contain tiny otoliths ("ear stones"). When your head tilts, the otoliths shift and press against hair cells, providing information on your position. Each inner ear also contains three fluid-filled **semicircular canals**, arranged at right angles to one another. Whenever your head moves, the fluid moves in one of the semicircular canals and nerve messages transmitted to the brain give further information on your position and movement. On a moving boat or car, and especially in a spinning amusement park ride, the messages from the semicircular canals may change too rapidly for the brain's processing centers to keep up with them. Then you may suffer the dizzy, nauseous feelings of motion sickness.

This tiny device converts sounds to electrical signals. It may be surgically implanted in the ear to take the place of a damaged cochlea.

TASTE AND SMELL

What is your favorite food? Whether your answer is chocolate ice cream, a sizzling steak, a juicy peach, a slice of pizza, or some other treat, you'll have picked something whose taste you really love.

Small groups of sensory cells on your tongue, called **taste buds**, react to the chemicals in foods. Humans have taste buds that react to four main tastes: sweet, sour, salty, and bitter. The flavors of foods are combinations of these four basic tastes. In general, sugars and alcohols have sweet tastes, acids are sour, salts taste salty, and alkaloids are bitter.

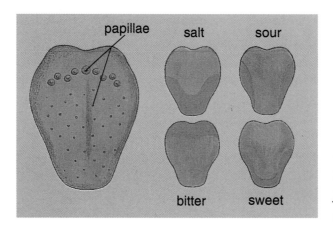

Location on the tongue of the taste buds for salt, sour, bitter, and sweet tastes

Sensory messages from the taste buds are sent first to the brain stem and then on to the thalamus. From there they are relayed up to the taste areas in the cortex of the parietal lobes. Meanwhile, the taste pathways in the brain stem are also linked with the salivary glands. Your saliva begins to flow when you taste food—and also when you smell or even think about something you know will taste good.

People don't always agree about which foods taste good or bad. Some people love eggs or spinach or liver, while others hate them. Part of the reason for these differences may be that the same foods actually don't taste the same to everyone. In fact, scientists have found chemicals, such as PTC (phenylthiocarbamide), that taste bitter to some people but others—up to 30 percent of the population—can't taste them at all. Being a PTC taster or nontaster is hereditary. A lot of the difference, though, is the result of experience. If a food makes you ill, you will very likely dislike its taste afterward. Most people find bitter tastes unpleasant, which is probably a protective mechanism inherited from our ancestors who avoided bitter-tasting poisonous plants. Yet you can learn to like tastes you used to find unpleasant.

Our sense of taste is closely linked with our sense of smell. Have you ever noticed how bland things taste when your nose is stuffed up by a cold? A postage stamp-sized patch of **olfactory cells** in the mucous membrane lining each nostril reacts to chemicals in the air and sends sensory messages to the brain. Scientists have tried to draw up lists of primary smells, like the three primary colors and four primary tastes, but their lists do not agree very well. One smell classification listed seven main olfactory stimulants, including musk, floral, and peppermint, but other researchers believe there may be as many as 50 or more primary smells. People can distinguish among more than 10,000 different smells.

Sensory messages from the olfactory cells are transmitted directly to the olfactory bulbs, a pair of cranial nerves that are actually outgrowths from the base of the brain. From there one main nerve pathway leads into the hypothalamus, the amygdala, and other parts of the limbic system. The "smell brain" is one of the most ancient parts of our central nervous system, and odors are closely linked with emotions. They also contribute to the formation of very strong memories. Another nerve pathway leads up into the cerebral cortex, where the conscious analysis of odors occurs.

Among many of our animal relatives, smell plays an important role in mating. Animals recognize one another by characteristic body odors and are attracted by **pheromones**, hormonelike chemicals that are sent out into the air to be smelled by other animals and influence their behavior. These pheromones are perceived by a special sensory organ in the nose, called the vomeronasal organ (VNO). Recently the VNO has been found in humans also, and there is some evidence that we, too, produce and react to pheromones.

TOUCH

Can you identify an object just by touch? If you have a friend place something in your hand, you will be able to tell a lot about it even with your eyes closed. Your fingers will tell you whether it is hard or soft, smooth or rough, wet or dry or sticky. You will know by feel how big it is, and its general shape.

The skin has nerve endings specialized for gathering sensory information. Some of these receptors are sensitive to heat and cold. Others are sensitive to touch, pressure, or pain. The touch receptors respond to the slightest contact. You can feel an ant walking across your hand. Pressure and pain receptors have a **threshold**: they do not react unless the stimulus is strong enough. There are three to four million pain receptors in your skin, but only 500,000 touch receptors. Most of the touch receptors are found in your fingers, tongue, and lips. In parts of the body such as the back, they are spaced so widely that if you asked a friend to poke you in the back you would not be able to tell without looking whether one, two, or three fingers were pressed against your skin.

The skin sense receptors are typically able to adapt: when a stimulus continues for a while at the same strength, the receptors send fewer and fewer messages to the brain. Touch receptors adapt very quickly. That is a good thing; otherwise, you would be constantly bothered by the feel of your clothes—and even your own hair—against

Touch receptors in our fingers are very sensitive.

your skin. Temperature receptors also adapt fairly quickly. When you first dive into a pool the water may seem icy cold, but soon it feels comfortable. A bath may feel too hot at first, but after a few minutes it just seems warm, and then you stop noticing its temperature at all. Pressure and pain receptors adapt much more slowly, and that is a good thing, too. Something that is pressing hard against your skin may cause damage, and something painful may already be damaging your body. Feelings of discomfort and pain are warning signals to prompt you to do something about a dangerous situation.

When one of the sensory nerve pathways from the skin is stimulated, the brain perceives the feeling as coming from the skin, no matter where the actual stimulation is occurring. If your arm "goes to sleep" because you were resting your head on it, you feel the numbness and later the "pins and needles" pains in your hand, not in the upper arm where you were pressing on the nerves. The basic awareness of pain occurs in the thalamus, but pain messages are also transmitted to the cerebral cortex, which localizes the pain and recognizes its type and intensity.

Various drugs can be used to relieve pain. Aspirin, for example, works by stopping the production of prostaglandins, chemicals that stimulate pain sensations. Morphine and other opiates stop the transmission of pain messages by binding to chemical receptors on nerve cells in the brain and spinal cord. Researchers have discovered that the body produces natural morphinelike painkillers, called **endorphins**. They think that people who can tolerate more pain than the average may produce more endorphins. These chemicals are also produced during strenuous exercise and are believed to be responsible for the "runner's high" that some long-distance runners experience.

Pain-relieving drugs are called analgesics. Anesthetics are drugs that block sensation in general. Local anesthetics, injected near the site of an operation, block the transmission of pain messages to the brain. General anesthesia—using drugs that are injected or inhaled—stops the perception of pain by causing unconsciousness.

REGENERATING NERVES

From time to time there are stories in the newspaper about a person who has had a hand or other body part successfully reattached when it was cut off by accident. Such an operation requires hours of delicate work by surgeons, who must carefully match up and suture dozens of blood vessels, ligaments, and other structures. After the operation, it will be many months before it is known whether the use of the hand has been fully restored.

The peripheral nerves leading down into the hand have been cut, and unless they regenerate successfully, the replaced hand will not be able to move properly and may be without sensation.

When nerves are damaged by injury or disease, the damage is sometimes reversible. Within 24 hours after injury, little buds begin to appear at the end of the cut nerve. They lengthen out into fibers, and branch and grow together with the other cut end. But the process can take as long as a year or two to complete.

Sympathetic fibers are the first to regenerate. The first sign of a return of function to the affected part is usually an improvement in skin color, as the nerves that supply the blood vessels are restored.

Sensory fibers are restored next, with a return of sensitivity first to pressure or pinching, then to pain, heat and cold, and finally to joint movements and touch localization. Motor function is the last to be restored.

But the recovery is usually not perfect. The fibers might not connect in the right places. A motor fiber, for example, that had formerly controlled the muscle that bends the little finger, might wind up controlling a muscle that moves the thumb. Sensory messages might also become mixed up. This confuses the brain, which had relied on a lifetime of past experience to determine which impulses belong to which part of the body. The brain can relearn to recognize these new impulse patterns, but it is a long process, and it is usually more successful the younger the patient is at the time of the injury.

For a long time it was thought that only peripheral nerves could regenerate, and damage to the spinal cord would result in irreversible paralysis (the loss of movement or sensation). But New York Giants defensive end Dennis Byrd, who was paralyzed by a broken neck in an accidental collision with a teammate late in 1992, was walking unaided a year later. He had the benefit of two experimental drugs: methylprednisolone, a steroid hormone, and GM-1, a growth-promoting substance naturally found in nerve cell membranes.

PARALYSIS ON PURPOSE

Temporarily interrupting the passage of impulses along a nerve path can be produced in a variety of ways. Some are useful to stop pain. Applying ice to the skin in a place where the nerve passes near the surface causes a nerve block. Pressing on a nerve for 20 minutes or more produces anesthesia of the part of the body that the nerve serves. This is what happens when your foot goes to sleep when you sit on it. If the pressure is continued too long, the paralysis becomes irreversible. A number of chemicals act as local anesthetics, blocking nerve transmission, when injected into the area around the nerve.

PROBLEMS

When things go wrong with the brain, it can be a very serious problem because the brain controls the entire body. The brain can be injured in an accident or because of an illness or disease.

Some children are born with hereditary conditions such as Down syndrome, which prevent them from learning as quickly as other children.

Cerebral palsy is a condition due to a developmental defect or damage to the brain during birth. It is characterized by spastic paralysis, muscular incoordination, and often a severe speech impediment. This disorder generally affects the motor areas of the brain, and the person's intelligence is usually normal or even above normal.

Huntington's disease is a hereditary disorder that usually does not show any effects until middle age. It causes various parts of the cerebrum to wither away. Early symptoms are involuntary jerky movements. Eventually Huntington's disease leads to an irreversible loss of mental abilities.

Multiple sclerosis is a disease of the central nervous system characterized by hardening of patches of connective tissue in the brain and spinal cord. Some of the axons in the brain and spinal cord lose their myelin sheaths and cannot conduct nerve impulses effectively. Symptoms get progressively worse, with general weakness, muscular incoordination, and blurring of vision, ending in death.

Sometimes a child is born with a skull that is far larger than a normal newborn's. This is a serious sign that, if left unchecked, can result in severe brain damage. Water on the brain is caused by an excess of cerebrospinal fluid inside the skull. If the fluid is allowed to accumulate, it flattens the brain into a thin shell against the skull.

Bacteria and viruses can also cause nervous system problems. Viruses such as the poliomyelitis virus (which causes polio) may attack the brain or spinal cord. Before a polio vaccine was developed, polio was never one of the major killers, but it left its victims—usually young children—paralyzed and crippled for life.

Encephalitis, an inflammation of the brain caused by another virus, produces lethargy and drowsiness. Meningitis is an inflammation of the meninges in the cranium or spine. It can be caused by infection by bacteria, viruses, or fungi and is often characterized by fever, pain in the back and limbs, and paralysis.

In Parkinson's disease, neuron pathways in the brain may be destroyed. Then patients have difficulty doing the things they were always able to do. They may move around very slowly, and their hands might tremble.

Epilepsy may occur when the electrical activity in the brain is not normal. During an epileptic seizure, a person may fall to the ground and shake all over. People with epilepsy usually do not realize they are having a seizure while it is occurring.

A **tumor** is a swelling somewhere in the body that is caused by a sudden growth of cells. Some tumors are dangerous because they keep on growing, destroying tissue all around them—they are said to be malignant tumors. Others are not as dangerous because they stop growing and will not spread—these are benign tumors. However, any tumor in the brain can be dangerous because it might press on important parts of the brain.

Damage to the nervous system may occur by traumatic injury—a skull fracture, for example, may drive bone splinters into the brain or cause a part of the skull to press on the cerebrum. Crushing of vertebrae may pinch or sever the spinal cord, affecting the nerves that are served by the parts of the spine below the injury. Damage to certain parts of the brain and spinal cord can cause paralysis, a loss of motor function, or anesthesia, the loss of sensation.

A person whose brain is too badly damaged by disease or an accident will die. But sometimes only a part of the brain is damaged. Then the person will not be able to do things that are controlled by that part of the brain. However, he or she may be able to relearn or retrain the brain and body so that another part of the brain takes over control of the ability that was lost. New pathways can be formed in the healthy parts of the brain.

A stroke may occur when the blood supply to a part of the brain is cut off. A stroke victim may lose the ability to use parts of one side of the body. With exercise and training a person can relearn skills that have been lost.

Fainting is a brief loss of consciousness, which lasts only a few seconds

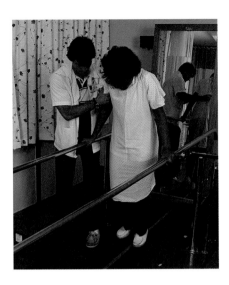

A stroke victim learning how to walk again with the aid of a physical therapist

or minutes. It may result from a blow on the head, or from pooling of blood in the lower extremities, or it may be a symptom of disease.

A **coma** is a state of unconsciousness in which the person is totally unable to respond to stimuli. It may result from head injury, disease, poison, or some chemical imbalance in the body. A coma may last for only a few minutes, or for days, or much longer. After recovering from a coma, the person may experience **amnesia**, a loss of memory.

Concussion is a bruising of the brain caused by a violent blow to the head, usually resulting in a brief period of unconsciousness. Reversible damage to the brain stem centers may be involved, and the regaining of consciousness may be followed by a temporary amnesia.

Headache is the most common of all central nervous system disorders. The next time you have a headache, you might reflect that it is actually not your brain that is hurting, since the nerve cells of the brain are insensitive to pain. Most headaches are due to swollen blood vessels in the head, spasms of the scalp muscles, or stretching or irritation of the meninges.

Headaches can occur for a wide variety of reasons including a toothache, a bad cold that blocks up the sinuses, eyestrain, tiredness, constipation, or a poison such as alcohol, which irritates the meninges. It can also be a sign of a serious disorder such as a brain tumor. Most headaches do not last very long, but some can last or recur over a period of months or years. Headaches may also have psychological causes; they may be caused by emotional tension, for example. A common and especially painful type of headache is the **migraine**, which is often preceded or accompanied by visual effects such as spots before the eyes and an extreme sensitivity to light. The pain may occur on only one side of the head.

Doctors can cure some types of brain problems with surgery or medicine. Some may clear up quickly, but others such as epilepsy and Parkinson's disease can be helped, but not yet cured.

Surgeons may remove a tumor or repair other damage to the brain by operating. In order to find out more clearly what the problem is, doctors have ways of looking inside the brain before they operate. Machines called scanners are very useful tools in helping doctors decide what needs to be done.

X rays (high-energy radiations that we cannot see) may show a tumor or other problem. The CAT (computerized axial tomography) scanner uses X rays to take pictures of the brain. It allows doctors to see many layers of brain tissue. The MRI (magnetic resonance imaging) scanner also gives a picture of a "slice" of the brain, but it does not use X rays. It is based on changes produced in the nuclei of atoms in the magnetic fields generated by radio waves. Doctors using these scanners can find out which parts of the brain were damaged after a stroke or determine where a tumor is located.

PET (positron emission tomography) scanners can show the brain in action. Radioactively labeled sugarlike compounds are injected into the bloodstream and tend to accumulate in the parts of the brain that are active. Mental activity uses energy, normally provided in the form of glucose. Studies using PET scanners have revealed striking differences in the brains of people with mental illnesses such as schizophrenia.

Tests on samples of cerebrospinal fluid can also provide valuable clues to what is going on in the central nervous system. Samples are obtained by lumbar puncture: drawing fluid out of the spinal canal with a hollow needle inserted through the gap between vertebrae in the back.

Neurosurgeons are doctors who operate on the brain and nerves. An American doctor named Harvey Cushing performed the first successful brain surgery in 1905. Since that time doctors have come a long way in helping people with brain problems. Today there are many new tools to aid in brain surgery. For example, doctors can use strong light rays called lasers to remove damaged parts of the brain without cutting into normal surrounding tissue. Now they are able to save many people who have brain tumors.

DISEASES OF THE MIND

More people suffer from mental illnesses than from all other diseases. The human brain is so complicated and so delicate that many things can go wrong with it—and when they do, the results can be very strange. People with a mental illness may see or hear things that are not really there. This is called a hallucination. They may think that people are trying to hurt them all the time, and they may turn against those who love them and are really trying to help them. This is called **paranoia**.

Mental illness can be very mild, so mild that the person who suffers from it can get along almost normally in the world. For example, some people have compulsions. There are people who feel that their hands are never clean, and they must wash them 100 times a day or more. Other people have irrational fears, or **phobias**: they may be terrified to ride in airplanes or in elevators or afraid of being in a crowd or in a closed room. But if they can manage to avoid the things they fear, they can usually get along all right. Such mild forms of mental illness are sometimes called **neuroses**.

Other forms of mental illness are more serious. Everyone gets depressed once in a while, when things are going badly. But they soon feel better. A person suffering from clinical **depression**, however, feels sad all the time, even when things seem to be going well. Depression can be triggered by a tragedy that the person can't seem to handle, such as a death in the family. Many researchers believe that severe depression can result from an imbalance of neurotransmitters in the brain—a deficiency of dopamine, norepinephrine, and serotonin—and that it is hereditary.

People suffering from **mania** may be filled with uncontrollable enthusiasm, causing them to do things that may seem "crazy," such as constantly talking, making unrealistic grand plans, and going on excessive shopping sprees. This, too, may be a hereditary condition and seems to be linked with an overproduction of dopamine, norepinephrine, and serotonin (the same neurotransmitters that are lacking during depression).

Some people continually go through cycles, seesawing between mania and depression. People with this condition, called manic-depressive or bipolar disorder, often have lower than normal amounts of the mineral lithium in their blood, and lithium treatments help many of them to live more normally. But some researchers have pointed out that many very intelligent and creative people have been manic-depressive.

Very serious forms of mental illness are often called **psychoses**. People who suffer from these diseases are so concerned with their fears or imaginings that they cannot live normally. They may completely lose contact with the real world around them and live in an imaginary world of their own. People suffering from schizophrenia, for example, may sit for hours on end, dully staring into space. Or they may fly into sudden rages—perhaps spurred on by "voices" that no one else can hear—and hurt themselves or others. Someone with dementia (severe mental impairment associated with brain damage) may be unable to remember things or perform simple tasks.

It was once thought that senility was a normal part of aging. As senility progresses, there is a gradual loss of memory and the ability to reason clearly and learn new things. Eventually, the ability to do the daily tasks required to live independently is lost. Most of the body systems gradually grow less efficient, after all, and the nervous system is particularly vulnerable because nerve cells that die are not replaced. But people age at different rates. Some begin to show signs of senility in their fifties or sixties; others are still vigorous and mentally sharp in their eighties, nineties, or beyond.

One major type of senile dementia is Alzheimer's disease, the causes of which are still a mystery. The brains of people with Alzheimer's show characteristic changes, such as tangled masses of nerve fibers and a deficiency of the neurotransmitter acetylcholine and the neurons that secrete it.

Doctors have discovered that in many cases what appears to be senility is actually the result of some other, treatable condition. Memory loss and confusion may be the result of depression, vitamin deficiencies, hearing loss, or overmedication for high blood pressure, for example.

TREATING MENTAL ILLNESS

Psychology is the study of the mind and how it works. It comes from a Greek word for "soul" or "life." Psychologists study how people feel, act, think, learn, understand, remember, and forget. They try to understand how we behave and figure out what is normal behavior for children and adults and what is abnormal. Psychiatrists are medical doctors who have specialized in the study and treatment of mental illness.

What causes mental illness? Some psychiatrists believe that bad experiences when one was a child can be the cause of mental illness later in life. But this theory does not explain why many children who have even worse experiences grow up to be normal adults.

Scientists are now coming to believe that the secrets of mental illness lie in the chemistry of the brain. There is evidence that schizophrenics' brains produce too much dopamine, as well as other chemicals that can affect mental functions. (Chemicals taken from the urine of schizophrenic patients, when injected into normal people, can make them act "crazy.")

Poisons such as mercury can produce symptoms resembling mental illness. Deficiencies of certain substances in the diet, such as B vitamins, can also have an effect on the brain and make people act strangely, just as though they suffered from a neurosis or psychosis. These symptoms clear up when the patient is placed on a proper diet.

Group counseling sessions help some people to talk about their problems.

Many people who suffer from mental illnesses are able to get by in their lives. Some are helped by talking about their problems with friends or psychiatrists, psychologists, or other counselors. The Austrian doctor Sigmund Freud is famous for inventing the technique of psychotherapy. Patients talk about their problems, either in a group or one-on-one with a psychiatrist. Medications may be prescribed to help correct balances of brain chemicals. Antidepressants, for example, work by increasing the amounts of neurotransmitters available in the brain. Many tranquilizers used for schizophrenia and other psychological disorders work by blocking the brain's dopamine receptors.

BE A TRUE FRIEND

If you have a friend who is depressed and talks about suicide, don't wait...TELL a trusted parent, teacher, or other adult. That is the first step in getting help for your friend.

Telling may save a life!

DRUGS AND THE MIND

Drug abuse is a major concern in today's world. And yet, many people who would never dream of taking an illegal drug use mind-altering substances each day. Coffee, tea, and cola drinks all contain caffeine, a stimulant drug. Chocolate contains smaller amounts of caffeine, together with theobromine, a chemical with similar effects. Cigarettes deliver doses of nicotine, a powerful drug that is classified as a stimulant but can also have relaxing effects. Another widely used (and abused) legal drug is alcohol, taken in the form of beer, wine, and liquor.

There are three main groups of drugs that alter the workings of the brain. **Stimulants** increase the activity of the central nervous system and promote feelings of energy and high spirits. **Depressants** lower the level of central nervous system activity, but they don't necessarily make a person feel depressed. Instead, by removing the normal **inhibitions**, they usually produce a high. The third main group, **psychedelics**, includes various mind-altering substances that can change and distort perceptions.

Mind-altering drugs often produce **tolerance**—that is, a person who has been taking the drug for a while needs larger amounts to produce the same effect. Most of these drugs are **addictive**: they alter brain and body chemistry so that the user can no longer get along without regular doses. Stopping the use of an addictive drug leads to withdrawal, which can range from headaches and irritability to hallucinations, convulsions, and even death.

Taken in moderation, caffeine is a relatively harmless stimulant. But in larger amounts it can cause nervousness, irritability, and sleep disorders; withdrawal may mean a day or two of headaches.

Cigarette smoking is another legal form of drug use. It can cause lung cancer, due to the tars in the smoke. Smoking can also lead to cancer of the mouth and throat, and chewing tobacco can cause cancer of the mouth. Further studies have shown that nicotine can contribute to heart disease.

Cocaine is a stimulant drug that is far from harmless. It produces a rush of euphoria that may be followed by deep depression and a craving for more of the drug. A large dose of cocaine can sometimes result in a fatal heart attack or stroke, even in a young, healthy person.

Amphetamines, another group of stimulants that are abused, increase the available amounts of the neurotransmitter norepinephrine, making the user's brain overexcited. Amphetamine users may become unstable and suffer from hallucinations and paranoia.

Alcohol is still the most frequently abused depressant drug. The immediate effects of alcohol include not only a pleasant high but also various degrees of slurring of speech, slowing of reactions, and difficulty in coordinating movements. Long-term abuse can lead to health problems such as liver damage and devastating effects on the user's personal life.

Narcotics are highly addictive depressant drugs and include heroin, opium, morphine, and codeine. They bind to the brain's opiate receptors, which normally would hold the natural endorphins. When the receptors are occupied by narcotics, the brain cuts back its production of endorphins. As drug use continues, more receptors are produced and more of the drug is needed to fill them and produce a high. If drug use is stopped, the receptors are freed and pain messages are sent to the conscious part of the brain. That is the reason for withdrawal. Methadone, a synthetic narcotic, can be used as a treatment for heroin addiction because it binds to the same receptors (thus blocking heroin's effects) but does not produce a high.

Barbiturates are also highly addictive depressant drugs that can be abused. They are sometimes prescribed as sleeping medications, but they are really not very good sleeping pills because they suppress REM sleep.

The psychedelics include a number of natural substances, such as mescaline (from peyote), psilocybin (from psilocybe mushrooms), nutmeg, and marijuana (from cannabis, the hemp plant). In some cultures these drugs are used to produce visions, as a part of religious ceremonies.

Someone who takes LSD, a synthetic psychedelic, sees the world differently. Shapes and sounds become distorted, and hallucinations may occur. Sometimes this is a pleasant experience, but often it is like a nightmare haunted by frightening demons. The symptoms caused by LSD are very similar to those experienced by a patient with schizophrenia.

LIFE AND DEATH AND THE BRAIN

The brain uses a lot of energy to do its job. It needs a large oxygen supply for its energy needs. If a neuron goes as much as ten seconds without oxygen, it may die. After about four minutes without oxygen, the whole brain may die.

If your brain isn't getting enough oxygen, you will feel a bit dizzy and then might faint, briefly losing consciousness. If you still don't get enough oxygen you may remain unconscious. When a person goes into a deep unconsciousness it is called a coma.

In the past, a person was considered to be dead when his or her heart stopped working. But nowadays the definition of death is a little harder to

PUSHING THE TIME LIMIT

When a person's face is suddenly plunged into cold water, a reflex action slows down the body's metabolism, so that the brain and other organs need less oxygen than usual. This "diving reflex," which we share with seals and other water animals, has saved some people from drowning even though they were underwater for far longer than the four minutes the brain can normally live without oxygen.

A harbor seal

pin down. Heart attacks, strokes, and various kinds of injuries may cause a person's vital organs—the heart and lungs—to stop working. But doctors can keep the person alive by using machines to take the place of the heart and lungs until the damage can be repaired.

Now in many states, "brain death" has become the accepted definition of death. This condition is determined by the absence of electrical activity in the brain, as shown by a flat EEG. But doctors and legislators are still not in full agreement on exactly what brain death means. In some states it is taken to mean no brain waves from the cerebral cortex, but in others there must also be no activity from the brain stem, which controls many basic life functions. Yet a person with brain stem activity but no cerebral cortex activity could never regain consciousness. He or she would never be able to read, speak, or understand anything. So, does such a definition of death mean that parents of a child born without a cerebrum cannot donate their baby's organs for transplants to save other babies' lives? Would it be murder to turn off the life support machinery for an accident victim who has only brain stem activity? Debate on bioethical questions like these is still going on.

GLOSSARY

addiction—a condition in which the brain and body chemistry have been altered by a drug so that the user can no longer function normally without regular doses of it.

adrenaline—a hormone produced by the adrenal glands; its effects are similar to those of the sympathetic nervous system.

amnesia—a loss of memory.

amygdala—limbic system structures just above the pituitary gland, which relay experiences involving emotions to other parts of the brain.

arachnoid membrane—the thin, delicate middle membrane of the meninges.

autonomic nervous system—the nerves that carry out various automatic functions, such as regulating breathing, which are not usually under conscious control.

axon—a long, threadlike part of a neuron that transmits impulses away from the cell body. It ends in a cluster of terminal branches.

backbone—a flexible column made up of interlocking bones (vertebrae), which protects the spinal cord; also called spinal column or vertebral column.

brain—a central controlling and coordinating organ of the nervous system.

brain stem—the lower part of the brain, consisting of the midbrain and hindbrain.

brain waves—the patterns of electricity generated by the brain's activity.

cell body—the portion of a neuron containing the nucleus and other typical cell structures.

central nervous system—the brain and spinal cord.

cerebellum—a hindbrain structure that coordinates movements and balance.

cerebral cortex—the outermost layer of the cerebrum; the "thinking" portion of the brain.

cerebrospinal fluid—a clear liquid that fills the brain ventricles, the channel inside the spinal cord, and the space between the inner and middle meninges.

cerebrum—the thinking brain, involved with conscious perception, voluntary actions, memory, thought, and personality.

cochlea—a coiled, fluid-filled tube in the inner ear, containing cells sensitive to sound vibrations.

colliculi—midbrain structures that help to control and adjust the eyes and ears.

coma—a state of deep unconsciousness, in which the person cannot respond to stimuli.

concussion—bruising of the brain caused by a violent blow on the head, usually resulting in brief unconsciousness.

conditioned reflex—a learned reflex action prompted by a stimulus that was associated with the natural stimulus for the reflex.

connector neurons—nerve cells in the brain or spinal cord that connect two other neurons.

convolutions—the ridges (gyri) and furrows (sulci or fissures) on the surface of the cerebrum and cerebellum.

corpus callosum—a thick cable of nerve fibers at the base of the brain that links the two cerebral hemispheres.

cranial nerves—twelve pairs of peripheral nerves that branch out from the brain.

cranium—a hard, helmetlike bony covering that protects the brain; also called the skull.

dendrites—threadlike branches of a neuron that carry impulses toward the cell body.

depressants—drugs that lower the level of central nervous system activity and remove inhibitions, which may produce a "high."

depression—a condition in which a person feels sad and hopeless. It may be caused by external circumstances. Clinical depression is a mental illness in which the sad feelings persist for a long time, without any objective cause. It may be the result of a chemical imbalance in the brain.

diencephalon—a portion deep inside the brain containing the thalamus, hypothalamus, and pineal gland; also called the 'tweenbrain.

dura mater—the tough, outermost membrane of the meninges.

EEG (electroencephalograph)—a machine that records brain wave patterns.

endocrine glands—structures that produce hormones and secrete them into the bloodstream.

endorphins—natural brain chemicals with a morphinelike painkilling effect.

faint—a brief temporary loss of consciousness due to an insufficient supply of oxygen to the brain.

forebrain—the cerebrum and structures of the 'tweenbrain (diencephalon) including the thalamus and hypothalamus.

frontal lobes—the part of the cerebrum at the front, in the forehead area.

ganglia—masses of nerve cells bunched together.

glial cells—cells that support and nourish neurons; also called neuroglia.

gray matter—brain tissue consisting of nerve cells without myelin sheaths.

hallucination—a sense perception of something that is not there.

hemispheres—the two halves of the cerebrum.

hindbrain—the medulla oblongata, pons, and cerebellum.

hippocampus—a limbic system structure necessary for the formation of long-term memories.

hypothalamus—a portion of the brain containing many control centers for body functions and emotions; it regulates the pituitary gland's secretions.

impulse—a message transmitted along nerve cells.

inhibition—the prevention of an action.

intelligence—a complex set of mental abilities including memory, learning, and problem solving.

limbic system—regions of the brain concerned with emotions; includes the thalamus, hypothalamus, amygdala, hippocampus, and parts of the cerebrum.

mania—a condition characterized by uncontrollable enthusiasm, high energy, rapid speech, and a tendency to make grand, unrealistic plans.

medulla oblongata—the portion of the brain stem just above the spinal cord. It contains control centers for heartbeat, breathing, and digestion.

memory—a record of facts or events, stored in the brain. Short-term memory is a temporary record of events of the last few minutes; long-term memory is a permanent record, believed to be stored in the form of nerve pathways.

meninges—membranes that surround and protect the brain and spinal cord.

midbrain—the portion of the brain connecting the hindbrain and forebrain; also called mesencephalon.

migraine—a type of headache that typically affects one side of the head and may be preceded by visual effects such as spots before the eyes.

mixed nerves—nerves that contain both sensory and motor nerve fibers.

motor end plates—the buttonlike endings of motor nerves.

motor nerves—nerves that carry messages from the brain to the muscles, glands, and other body structures, resulting in actions.

motor strips—portions of the cerebral cortex controlling voluntary actions.

motor unit—a motor neuron and the muscle fibers it controls.

muscle spindles—proprioceptors that report to the brain when muscle fibers stretch.

myelin sheath—a shiny, white, insulating covering over some nerve fibers.

narcotics—depressant drugs derived from the opium poppy that act at the brain's endorphin receptors and relieve pain and/or produce a "high."

nerve fibers—axons and dendrites.

nerve net—a network of nerves found in lower animals such as coelenterates.

neurilemma—a covering over nerve fibers, made up of living cells.

neuromuscular junction—the meeting point of a motor nerve ending and a muscle fiber.

neuron—a nerve cell.

neuroses—mild mental disorders in which behavior or perceptions are abnormal but the person is still able to live relatively normally.

neurotransmitter—a chemical that carries a nerve impulse across a synapse.

occipital lobes—the part of the cerebrum at the back of the head.

olfactory cells—smell receptors in the mucous membrane lining the nose.

olfactory nerves—cranial nerves carrying sensory messages for smell.

optic nerves—cranial nerves carrying sensory messages for vision.

paralysis—loss of motor function or sensation.

paranoia—a mental disorder in which the person imagines he or she is being persecuted.

parasympathetic nervous system—the portion of the autonomic nervous system that regulates the body's normal activities.

parietal lobes—the portions of the cerebrum in the upper part of the head.

peripheral nervous system—the sensory and motor nerves that connect the brain and spinal cord to the rest of the body.

pheromones—hormonelike chemicals with which animals communicate by smell.

phobias—irrational fears.

pia mater—the soft, delicate innermost membrane of the meninges.

pineal gland—a 'tweenbrain structure that acts as the body's "clock," regulating body rhythms.

pituitary gland—the "master gland" of the endocrine system, which controls and coordinates the secretions of other glands.

pons—the portion of the brainstem that links the medulla with the midbrain.

proprioceptors—sensory organs that report on the status of muscles and internal organs.

psychedelics—drugs that change and distort perceptions and may produce hallucinations.

psychoses—severe mental disorders that prevent sufferers from living normally.

RAS (reticular activating system)—a network of neurons running up through the brain stem into the thalamus and hypothalamus that acts as a central clearinghouse, determining which messages are important or novel enough to be sent on to the cerebral cortex.

reflex actions—automatic actions in reaction to a stimulus, performed very rapidly without conscious thought or decision.

reflex arc—the nerve pathway for a reflex action. It includes sensory, motor, and connector neurons.

REM sleep—a phase of sleep during which dreams occur and the eyes make rapid movements under the closed eyelids.

retina—a layer of light-sensitive cells lining the back of the eyeball.

semicircular canals—three fluid-filled curved tubes in the inner ear that provide information on position and movement.

sensory nerves—nerves that carry messages from sense receptors to the brain and spinal cord.

sensory strips—portions of the cerebral cortex that receive sensory information.

spinal cord—a long cord of nerves running through the spine (backbone) of vertebrate animals; it connects the brain with the rest of the body and controls some reflex actions.

spinal nerves—thirty-one pairs of peripheral nerves that branch out from the spinal cord.

steroids—a class of fatlike chemicals that include sex hormones and some of the adrenal hormones.

stimulants—drugs that increase the activity of the central nervous system and promote feelings of energy and high spirits.

stimulus—a signal that prompts an action.

stroke—cutoff of the blood supply to a part of the brain, resulting in death of brain cells and loss of speech or other functions.

sympathetic nervous system—the portion of the autonomic nervous system that prepares the body to cope with emergencies.

synapse—the gap between two neurons in a nerve pathway.

taste buds—taste sense receptors on the surface of the tongue.

temporal lobes—the portions of the cerebrum at the sides, above the ears.

thalamus—the brain's main relay station, which sends information to the cerebral cortex and other parts of the brain.

threshold—a limit below which a stimulus is not strong enough to produce a response.

tolerance—an adjustment of the body to a drug so that a higher dose is needed to produce the same effect.

tumor—a swelling caused by a sudden growth of cells. Malignant, or cancerous tumors grow uncontrollably; benign tumors stop growing and do not spread.

vertebra—one of the thirty-three bones that make up the spinal column. (Plural: vertebrae.)

vestibular complex—a portion of the medulla that helps to maintain balance.

white matter—brain tissue consisting of nerve cells covered by a myelin sheath.

TIMELINE

B.C.

400 Hippocrates (a Greek doctor) believed the brain had the power of thought and understanding and was involved in sense perception.

A.D.

160 Galen (Greek) showed the brain sent messages to the body through the spinal cord but thought movement was produced by "animal spirits."

1543 Andreas Vesalius (Belgian) published an anatomy book; suggested that thought and feelings came from the brain.

mid-1600s Jan Swammerdam (Dutch) showed muscles cause movement by contracting.

1770s Luigi Galvani (Italian) showed that electricity causes muscle contraction.

1790s Franz Gall (German) believed different parts of the body are controlled by different parts of the brain but thought bumps on the skull revealed personality traits (phrenology).

1873 Camillo Golgi (Italian) observed nerve cells for the first time after developing a special microscopy stain.

1861 Paul Broca (French) mapped a speech area in the left hemisphere of the brain.

1871 Carl Wernicke (German) found a different type of speech area in the brain.

mid-1870s Santiago Ramón y Cajal used Golgi's stain to prove the nervous system is made up of nerves.

1875 Richard Caton (English) first detected brain electricity (with implanted electrodes).

late 1800s Walther Nernst (German) suggested nerve messages are carried by electrochemical reactions.

early 1900s Sigmund Freud (Austrian) developed psychoanalysis.

1929 Hans Berger (German) detected brain waves from the skull surface and developed the EEG.

early 1950s Alan Hodgkin and Andrew Huxley described how nerve messages are transmitted.

1960s Roger Sperry (American) studied split-brain patients.

1970 Julius Axelrod (American), Ulf von Euler (Swedish), and Bernard Katz (British) shared a Nobel Prize for working out mechanisms of nerve transmission.

1972 American researchers at Johns Hopkins University discovered how morphine relieves pain and causes addiction.

1975 John Hughes and Hans Kosterlitz (Scottish) discovered endorphins.

1986 Rita Levi-Montalcini (Italian) and Stanley Cohen (American) shared a Nobel Prize for the discovery of nerve growth factors.

INDEX

intelligence, 63

jellyfish, 10

left hemisphere, 39,
    42–43, 68
long-term memory, 61

mania, 82–83
manic-depressive, 83
medulla oblongata, 22,
    23, 46–47
meninges, 25
meningitis, 79
mental illness, 84–85
midbrain, 13, 22,
    46–47, 71
migraine, 80
motor end plates, 66
motor unit, 66–67
movement, 66–67
MRI (magnetic reso-
    nance imaging), 81
multiple sclerosis, 78
muscle spindles, 66

Nernst, Walther
    Hermann, 15
nerve cells. *See* neurons.
nerve net, 10
neuroglia, 19
neuromuscular junction,
    66
neurons, 8, 18–19
    axon, 18
    cell body, 18
    connector neurons, 32
    dendrites, 18
    message travel, 28–31
    myelin sheath, 18
    nerve fibers, 18
    neurilemma, 18
    neuroses, 82
neurosurgeons, 81
neurotransmitter, 29

octopus, 11
occipital lobes, 39
olfactory cells, 73
olfactory nerves, 27
optic nerves, 27

pancreas, 57
paralysis, 14, 77, 79
paranoia, 82
parasympathetic nervous
    system, 53
parietal lobes, 39
Parkinson's disease, 79
Pavlov, Ivan, 33
peripheral nerves,
    26–27, 40, 76
peripheral nervous sys-
    tem, 16, 26
PET (positron emission
    tomography), 81
pheromones, 73
phobias, 82
pia mater, 25
pineal gland, 48
pituitary gland, 49, 56
polio, 78–79
pons, 22
proprioceptors, 66
psychiatrists, 84
psychologists, 84
psychology, 84
psychoses, 83
psychotherapy, 84
Purkinje cells, 44

Ramon y Cajal,
    Santiago, 15
reflexes
    conditioned reflex, 33
    connector neurons, 32
    reflex arc, 32
regenerating nerves,
    76–77
REM (rapid eye move-
    ment) sleep, 51

reticular activating sys-
    tem (RAS), 47
retina, 68, 69
right hemisphere, 39,
    42–43, 68

schizophrenia, 84, 85
semicircular canals, 71
senility, 83
short-term memory, 61
skull fracture, 79
spinal cord, 9, 16, 20,
    21, 24, 25
spinal nerves, 21
stimulus, 33
stroke, 35, 41, 42, 79
Swammerdam, Jan, 15
sympathetic nervous sys-
    tem, 53
synapse, 29

taste buds, 72
temporal lobes, 39, 71
tentacled hydra, 10
thalamus, 22, 48–49,
    58, 72
theta waves, 35
thyroid gland, 57
touch, 74–75
    receptor threshold, 74
tumor, 79

vertebrae, 20, 24–25,
    27, 81
    damage to, 79
Vesalius, Andreas, 14–15
vestibular complex, 46
virus, 78–79

whales, 12
white matter, 19, 38

X rays, 81

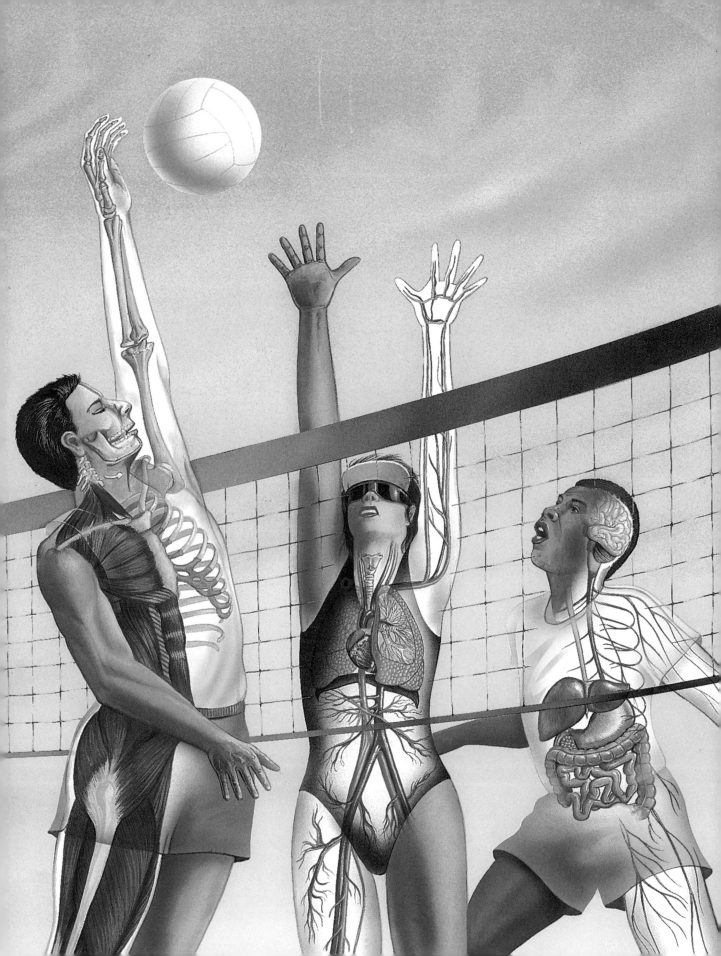

HEMET PUBLIC LIBRARY
510 E. FLORIDA AVE.
HEMET, CA 92543